THE INSIDER'S GUIDE TO
REAL ESTATE
INVESTING
LOOPHOLES

THE INSIDER'S GUIDE TO
REAL ESTATE INVESTING LOOPHOLES

Revised Edition

Diane Kennedy, CPA
Dolf de Roos, PhD

WILEY

John Wiley & Sons, Inc.

Published by John Wiley & Sons, Inc., Hoboken, New Jersey.
Published simultaneously in Canada.

For general information on our other products and services please contact our Customer Care Department within the United States at (800) 762-2974, outside the United States at (317) 572-3993 or fax (317) 572-4002.

Wiley also publishes its books in a variety of electronic formats. Some content that appears in print may not be available in electronic books. For more information about Wiley products, visit our web site at www.Wiley.com.

Designations used by companies to distinguish their products are often claimed by trademarks. In all instances where the author or publisher is aware of a claim, the product names appear in Initial Capital letters. Readers, however, should contact the appropriate companies for more complete information regarding trademarks and registration.

Library of Congress Cataloging-in-Publication Data:

Kennedy, Diane, 1956–
    The insider's guide to real estate investing loopholes / Diane Kennedy,
Dolf de Roos.—Rev. ed.
      p. cm.
    Rev. ed. of: The insider's guide to making money in real estate / Dolf de Roos and
Diane Kennedy. c2004.
    Includes index.
    ISBN 0-471-71179-9 (pbk.)
    1. Real estate investment.   2. Investments.   I. De Roos, Dolf.   II. De Roos, Dolf.
Insider's guide to making money in real estate.   III. Title.
HD1382.5.D468 2005
332.63'24—dc22   2004063709

Printed in the United States of America.
10 9 8 7 6 5 4 3

Acknowledgments

The authors would like to acknowledge the following people for their help with *The Insider's Guide to Real Estate Investing Loopholes*:

Richard Cooley

Megan Hughes

James Burgin

Mingoo Kang

Scott Mertens

Larry Jellen

Michael Hamilton

Laurie Harting

Alec Tanner

Elaine Harshbarger

Morgan Smith

Paul Wolf

Robert McCoy

Gabe Mendoza

Catrina Craft

Amy Fox

John Baen

Contents

CONTENTS

Introduction

Warning! The contents of this book may cause you to change your viewpoint toward taxes and investing. If you are ready to learn creative real estate investment techniques that put more money into your pocket through tax savings, then you'll want to keep this book close by. In fact, if that's your goal, consider buying three copies of this book: one copy for you, one copy for your CPA, and one copy for your real estate agent.

Since you are reading this, the chances are you're already a real estate investor or plan to be one soon. Both authors of this book are actively involved in real estate investing, as well as flipping, developing, and rehabbing, and we understand how valuable your time is. Let's face it—you could spend a day reading a book, or you could spend a day making thousands of dollars in another property transaction.

So because we understand what it takes to be a real estate investor, we want this book to be a resource that puts just as much money into your pocket as a property deal might. The money we can help you save is truly after-tax money. If you had a choice between making $10,000 (and paying tax at 40 percent) or saving $10,000 in taxes, our advice would be to take the tax savings! That's because the secret isn't always to make more money. Sometimes the secret is keeping more money. And saving on taxes is a great place to start.

WHAT IS A LOOPHOLE?

Many people think that the word *loophole* has inherent in it some implication of illegality. That is totally incorrect. A loophole is a government incentive to promote public policy. And one of the consistent government policies has been to promote real estate investing.

Humans have three essential needs—for food, clothing, and shelter. The government learned long ago that it does a horrible job of fulfilling the third fundamental need—shelter. Most of the time when the government has tried to get involved in providing housing, it has failed. Despite the fact that over the long term most real estate will increase in value, somehow the government's housing projects (tenements) almost always go down in value.

Yet housing continues to be an essential need, so government turned to the private sector to help those people in our society who have had trouble providing housing for themselves. To this end, the government encourages real estate investors by providing tax loopholes, which will provide government money to help meet this need.

So by investing in real estate and taking advantage of the loopholes to save taxes, you are actually doing exactly what the government wants you to do.

WHY DOESN'T EVERYONE KNOW ABOUT THIS?

Tax law is incredibly complex. Up until recently, only the rich were able to hire experienced professionals to create customized tax plans for them to exploit the available tax loopholes. But actually those loopholes are available to everyone, as long as they are willing to do what the government wants. *The Insider's Guide to Real Estate Investing Loopholes* discloses these loopholes that the rich know about and use.

MORE ABOUT *THE INSIDER'S GUIDE TO REAL ESTATE INVESTING LOOPHOLES*

To keep the information manageable, this book has been laid out in six parts. These six parts are: Basic Loopholes, Real Estate Loopholes, Home Loopholes, Creative Real Estate Investors, Easy Accounting for Real Estate Investors, and Global Investing.

Part I—Basic Loopholes

Did you ever consider that you could actually choose which tax laws you wanted? You can, you know. But first, you have to understand what all the taxes actually are, and then you can develop a plan to legally reduce their impact. We start off the first section with a review of which taxes impact investors in particular. Read **Part I—Basic Loopholes** to discover how an understanding of basic loopholes can transform your tax bill.

Part II—Real Estate Loopholes

The government has always made sure that the best loopholes are available just for real estate investors. In **Part II—Real Estate Loopholes,** we explain what those loopholes are. Learn how to turn a loss into an asset and how to use legal business structures to your advantage, to be smart with your debt, and to create the ultimate exit strategies. All this and more are disclosed in Part II—Real Estate Loopholes.

Part III—Home Loopholes

The best gift Congress ever gave us was in 1997, when the tax-free gain exclusion for single and married homeowners was introduced. And each year the IRS adds nuances that keep making it better. Use the home loopholes found in **Part III—Home Loopholes** to make your house pay you instead of the other way around.

Part IV—Creative Real Estate Investors

Real estate is a hot topic, and the past few years have seen a huge increase in the number of seminars, books, tapes, and other educational products touting the latest in creative real estate investing techniques. Often these techniques are simply new names for old ideas. Learn how to translate the creative strategies into real tax savings in **Part IV—Creative Real Estate Investors**.

Part V—Easy Accounting for Real Estate Investors

If there is one thing every new real estate investor soon discovers, it is that there is a lot of paperwork involved! To take maximum advantage of tax savings there are also some important rules on what to keep and how long to keep it. And, of course, there are some documents that your accountant will need to see each year. That information plus some simple steps to ensure you have what you need in case you are ever audited are all included in **Part V—Easy Accounting for Real Estate Investors**.

Part VI—Global Investing

Have you ever thought of investing outside the box of your own home country? If you're ready to add yet another dimension to your current investment strategies, you'll want to read **Part VI— Global Investing**. Maximize other countries' tax laws and currency trading to create an even more secure future for you and your family.

PART I

Basic Loopholes

Chapter 1

CHOOSE THE TAX LAWS YOU WANT

I f you had a choice of paying tax now or later, which one would you choose? How about if the government asked you whether you would like to pay tax equal to half of your income, or tax at a rate of 10 percent or less? The amazing thing is though, that this *is* exactly what the government asks us, each and every day. And we choose what tax we will pay, by the actions that we take.

If you choose to continue working at a job or in a profession where all of your income is earned by the work that you do, you will pay the highest rate. If you choose to work a little harder by taking another job or working overtime hours, your tax goes up along with the income you make. But, if instead you choose to invest in real estate and do that investing in conjunction with a tax plan, you will pay less tax.

First, though, let's look at how the tax system actually works.

WHY CAN'T I EVER GET A STRAIGHT ANSWER ON A TAX QUESTION?

Have you ever wondered why you can't get a straight answer to your tax question? Or worse, have you asked numerous people and gotten numerous answers? Why does this happen? The answer is quite simple. As we said earlier, tax law is complex.

Did you know that there are more than 500,000 pages of written tax law? (That makes it roughly 5,000 times as long as the Constitution!) And, what's more, tax law is constantly changing and being modified. Every day is a new day when it comes to taxes! Consider that there were more than 400 IRS Code changes for 2001. And for every code change, there are also one to five accompanying Treasury Regulations, Revenue Rulings, Revenue Procedures, and eventually multiple tax court cases. So more than 400 Code changes—and 2001 was considered a pretty uneventful year in the tax world! Now contrast that with years like 2002 when a new tax act came into play. In a busy year, you can have several thousand changes to the tax laws.

Now let's add another layer of complexity. There are three different key players in determining tax law: Congress, the IRS, and multiple district tax courts. Sometimes these different players don't agree. There are numerous instances of conflicting tax court opinions. And sometimes the code isn't even consistent within itself.

To make it even more complicated, tax law is comprised of "facts" and "opinions." A fact is something that can be proven to exist through physical evidence, while an opinion is something that may or may not be true. A tax fact is something that is so simple and clear-cut that there is only one answer. An example would be the instructions that tell us what line of our tax return form our income should go on. A tax opinion is much less clear.

It is based on an interpretation of facts, and it may or may not be true. An example of a tax opinion would be how much income needs to go on that line of our tax return form.

Most tax decisions are made based on opinion, which may or may not be true. Fortunately, there is a lot of guidance in tax law that helps informed and educated tax strategists make good decisions. The problem occurs when partially informed people try to make tax decisions. Tracking all of the tax law changes is a full-time job, and it is not something that a casual advisor can do well.

Believe it or not though, the worst answers of all can come directly from the IRS. Its agents are given only three days training before they are let loose on the Service Center telephones as "experts." IRS agents frequently don't even have accounting degrees. And if you get bad advice, the IRS is not liable for giving you that bad advice. In the late 1990s, the IRS did a much-publicized internal study of its own ability to answer questions. It discovered, to its chagrin, that the telephone questions were answered wrong almost 33 percent of the time. A recent internal study was done, a little more quietly this time, and it was discovered that questions are now answered wrong more than 40 percent of the time! And if you get the wrong answer, follow that advice, and are then later audited—you will pay tax, interest, and penalties.

To make matters worse, there are few CPAs who really understand real estate investment tax issues. The American Institute of Certified Public Accountants (AICPA) recently estimated that more than 80 percent of CPAs do not understand the basics of real estate tax issues.

So the bottom line is that we have a complicated set of tax laws, influenced by individual circumstances and understood by few. *The Insider's Guide to Real Estate Investing Loopholes* can help de-mystify tax law.

DO I REALLY NEED TO KNOW ALL THIS?

Well, yes and no. A major frustration for taxpayers is asking a question and being told that the answer is, "It depends." Accountants are famous for answering "it depends" to just about any question, but the fact is, the right plan really does depend on your own circumstances.

This is where you need to rely on your tax experts to further interpret the entire body of tax law based on what you want and need. It's not your job to be the tax expert (unless, of course, that really is your job). It is, however, your role to understand what they are talking about. Accountants, just like most other professionals, really do have their own language sometimes. If you want the best results, learn to speak their language.

QUICK-START GUIDE TO TAXES

So how do you become an expert on more than 500,000 pages of constantly changing tax law? Good news! There is actually a simple formula that explains how tax in the United States is calculated. It is called the Three Stage Tax Formula.

To do a Three Stage Tax Formula calculation, you:

- Report gross *income*.
- From gross income, you subtract *deductible expenses* to come to the amount of taxable income.
- Multiply the taxable income by the *tax rate* to determine the amount of tax.

It actually sounds quite simple, and a good tax strategy will encompass each of these stages. The key is to learn how you can manipulate each of these stages to your advantage, using IRS-approved loopholes.

■ **Income:** What is income? What are the different types of income? How can you change from one type of income to another and why does it matter? How can you turn taxable income into tax-deferred income or tax-free income?

■ **Expense:** What expenses are deductible? How can you make use of multiple business structures to create expenses on one side that are not income on the other? What personal expenses do you have now that are really hidden business deductions?

■ **Rate:** One of the best provisions that we have in the United States, and that many other countries do not have, is the ability to make use of a graduated tax rate. This means that there is not a flat tax rate applied to your taxable income. Instead, a portion of your income is taxed at one rate and then the next layer of income is taxed at a higher rate, and so on. If, for example, you have a tax rate of 28 percent for your personal return, this actually means that you have already filled up the income portions allowed at 10 percent and 15 percent, and for every additional dollar you make over these two amounts, you will pay 28 percent. So you aren't paying 28 percent on all of your income, only the amount that exceeds the 10 percent and 15 percent portions. We call 28 percent your marginal tax rate. Now how can you move income from your higher tax rate to a lower (or zero) tax rate?

A financial and tax strategy that incorporates real estate is the easiest way to impact ALL levels of the three stages—income, expenses, and tax rate. Real estate also allows an employee to deduct

---

Three Questions to Ask Yourself
(If You Really Want to Reduce Taxes)

Income: How can I change the type of income
             (earned, portfolio, or passive) I currently have
             to reduce taxes?

Expenses: What personal expenses do I have that might
             be hidden business deductions?

Tax Rate: How can I move my income to a lower tax
             rate?

---

many business expenses that normally would not be deducted against their wages. Finally, real estate, more than any other type of investment, has the widest range of tax law available to reduce, and even eliminate tax.

THREE BASKETS OF INCOME

Since the 1986 Tax Reform Act, the IRS has defined three different "baskets" of income. They are:

- Earned income—you work for the money.
- Passive income—your business or real estate works for you.
- Portfolio income—your money works for you.

Earned income is taxed at the ordinary tax rate. If you are self-employed but have the wrong business structure in place, you will also pay self-employment tax of 15.3 percent. If you were paid at the highest tax rate in 2004, that would mean a tax rate of more than 40 percent, for federal tax alone!

Portfolio income is usually in the form of long-term capital gains (assets sold after owning for more than one year) or dividends, and has a maximum rate of 15 percent.

Passive income such as that earned from real estate, if set up correctly, can receive cash flow with no tax whatsoever.

So based just on tax rates, it makes sense to move from earned income to portfolio or passive income. Real estate investing can help you do that!

There is one important thing to note about the three baskets of income, and that is there are many restrictions on losses and expenses that are incurred within these three categories. For example, you are limited in the amount of passive loss that you can take against earned income. You are similarly limited in the amount of portfolio loss (such as investment expenses or loss on sale of stock) that you can take against earned income.

REAL ESTATE LOSSES

Since 1986, U.S. tax laws have stated that losses can be claimed only against income in the same category. For example, passive losses can be used only against other passive income. You cannot take passive losses against earned income. Investment expenses, such as expenses for margin interest or investment education, can go only against portfolio income.

In the case of real estate the rules regarding passive losses are more complicated. If your income is less than $100,000, you are allowed to deduct up to $25,000 in losses from your real estate against other income. If you have more than $25,000 in losses, the excess amount is held as an unallowed loss until a future date when you sell the property. You don't forfeit the loss, but it's not very good tax planning to put off that loss to the future.

If your income is $100,000 or more, the amount of loss you can currently deduct is phased out. The unallowed loss is "suspended" against a future date when you sell the property. So the loss isn't "lost," but it is deferred. That's not great planning, either!

But, here's our first loophole, which will help you with this: Qualify as a real estate professional. If you are a real estate professional, you can take an unlimited amount of real estate losses against your other income.

TAXABLE INCOME

The three baskets of income are considered "taxable income." The IRS defines taxable income as "gross income" and says that "Except as otherwise provided . . . gross income means all income from whatever source derived." The best tax planning is in finding the loopholes that are defined within "except as otherwise provided."

For example, here's another great loophole available through real estate: Take money out of a property by refinancing. The cash you receive would not be taxable. Of course if you refinance, the payments on the property would go up. However, if you have been a responsible landlord, you will have been increasing the rents to offset the increased payments that would become due under a refinance.

On the other hand, what if you hadn't increased rents and couldn't get any additional rent from the property?

Say you refinanced a property and took out $100,000, intending to use that money for another investment. Your refinanced property now has additional mortgage costs of $7,500 per year. You used the $100,000 from the refinance to buy another building for $500,000. This building created a 15 percent cash-on-cash return in an area that had a conservative appreciation rate of 6 percent. After five years, using the refinancing loophole, here's what could happen:

Cash flow in new building = $7,500 ($15,000 minus mortgage payment of $7,500).

Cash flow total for five years: **$37,500**.

Appreciation = **$169,000** (after five years).

Total Increase: $206,500.

Wow! Debt can make you rich!

TAX-ADVANTAGED INCOME

The IRS has provided ways to take what would otherwise be taxable income and turn it into tax-deferred or tax-free income.

Tax-deferred income means that you put off having to pay tax until a later date. The benefit is that your money grows at a faster pace. For example, assume you pay tax at a 28 percent marginal tax rate and you earn $1,000 per year. After taking out money for taxes, you actually have only $720 available for future investment. On the other hand, if all of the amount can continue to grow, there is more available to grow. For example, if you invest that $1,000 per year at 12 percent for

20 years, the difference between paying tax each year and being able to defer that tax to a future date would mean an additional $6,456 in wealth. If you invested the $1,000 for 10 years, the difference is only $1,179. The unknown factors, of course, include the amount of interest you will earn and the future tax rate.

Tax-free income, on the other hand, means that not only does the investment grow without tax, but you can also liquidate that investment and take the value without paying tax on it. Obviously, tax-free income is the best way, wherever possible.

DEFERRED TAX

There are three ways to hold or transact real estate in a way that tax can be deferred. Sometimes you can even defer that tax forever!

1. *Installment Sale:* If you sell a property over time, that is called an installment sale. In other words, you will receive installments of payments over time. Each payment you receive is composed of at least two parts: (1) principal and (2) interest. The interest received will always be taxable just like any other portfolio income. However, in the case of the principal, it will actually be only partially taxable, depending on how it is apportioned between gain and return of capital.

   The calculation is important for two reasons. First, you are required to report the mortgage interest that you receive on a Form 1098 on an annual basis to the person paying you. Second, you will need that calculation to complete your year-end tax return. In both cases, I strongly recommend that you use a qualified accountant to prepare and calculate the forms, or at least use them to check your math!

A word of warning regarding installment sales. If the IRS considers you a real estate dealer (involved in the trade or business of real estate trading), you cannot qualify for installment sale treatment on payments. If you are a dealer, you must take all of the gain as taxable immediately. That means you could be in the position of paying tax on income you have not yet received! More on this in Chapter 2 "Tax Traps to Avoid."

2. *Buy real estate through your pension plan.* Some pension plans allow the purchase of real estate through your pension plan. There are some rules to follow about how you do it and some restrictions as to how the mortgages are handled, but there are a lot of benefits to doing your investing this way. For example, with a regular pension plan, the gain is deferred until you withdraw it from your pension plan. With a ROTH plan, you never pay tax. For more on this, see Chapter 2 "Tax Traps to Avoid."

3. *Section 1031—Like-Kind Exchange.* Currently, under U.S. tax law you can exchange real estate with someone else, in certain circumstances, and defer the gain that you would otherwise have to declare. The most common way to do this is through a "like kind," "Starker," or Section 1031 Exchange. These are all different ways of saying the same thing.

The like-kind exchange is described in IRC Section 1031 and further defined in a court ruling, *Starker* v. *Commissioner*; hence the other names. To keep things simple, we refer to the exchange as a "like-kind exchange." This is a specific exchange of real estate that has been owned for business or investment purposes. You cannot do a like-kind exchange (under this Code Section) on your personal residence or on non-real estate items. The like-kind exchange allows you to sell a piece of property that has appreciated, and "roll over" the gain into another piece of property. The second piece of property merely has to be another piece of business or investment real estate. It does not need to be the same type of investment property. You can exchange many properties into one property or vice versa. For example, you could exchange a single-family residence into an apartment building or a single-family residence into many single-family residences or bare land into two single-family residences. The possibilities are almost endless.

There are some rules for a like-kind exchange that must be closely followed. (See Chapter 7 "Sell Your Property without Immediately Paying Tax" for more details.) If you are considering a like-kind exchange, make sure you notify the real estate agent who is selling your property, as well as the title company. They will put you in touch with an exchange agent who will facilitate the sale and ensure the complex rules are followed.

Three Types of Income

Taxable—Tax Now

Tax Deferred—Tax Later

Tax Free—Tax Never

What type of income do you want?

WHY TYPE OF INCOME MATTERS

Once you understand what income is taxable and what type of income you have, you might find that you want to change the character of the income you receive.

Earned income means just that—you have to earn it. If your goal is financial freedom, which means the money you don't work for (your passive and portfolio income) exceeds your monthly expenses, then you want to turn earned income into the other forms. You can do that with your business, particularly if it is in the form of a C corporation. These strategies are covered in *Loopholes of the Rich—How the Rich Legally Make More Money and Pay Less Tax*. If you currently have a business producing income, you may want to discover the ways to change the type of income from your business (earned) into passive income through the use of real estate.

TAX RATE MAGIC

In real estate, there are even more opportunities to take advantage of lower tax rates due to special loopholes written for real estate investors and special capital gains treatment. Some of these advantages follow.

Tax-Free

We said earlier that tax-deferred income means that you will pay tax at a future date, whereas tax-free income means you will never pay tax. Obviously, tax-free income (as opposed to tax-deferred) is the way to go!

Much as with tax-deferred income; there are many different ways that you can have tax-free income. The first way is through a type of business or investment structure such as a ROTH IRA. The second way to produce tax-free income is through specific provisions within the current tax law as they pertain to real estate. The best example of that currently is with the tax-free gain that is allowed through the sale of your principal residence. You can now deduct $250,000 (if you are single) of gain on the sale of your home you have lived in for two of the past five years. If you are married, the exclusion amount jumps to $500,000. Chapter 10 "Be Paid to Live in Your Home" explains in more detail about how you can make use of this tax gift from Congress. Don't miss out on this exclusion!

Another way, often forgotten, is simply through refinancing. Think about it. If you own stock, about the only way to access an increase in value is to sell the stock. You've now got your cash, but have lost the appreciating (you hope) asset. But if you have real estate that has gone up in value and is likely to go up again, you can access the money through debt! We saw an example earlier in the chapter of how debt can make you rich. And you were able to get to that money to start that second investment without paying tax.

CAPITAL GAINS TAX

The tax rate for capital gains is less than the ordinary income tax rate. Unfortunately, tax law rarely is straightforward. The capital gains rate kicks in only when an asset is sold after a holding period of more than one year. Additionally, the gain is calculated using four key terms: sales price, basis, cost of selling, and accumulated depreciation. It's not simply a result of how much cash you end up with. We discuss this in greater detail in Chapter 16 "Accounting for the Sale."

OTHER TYPES OF TAX

The preceding review of tax planning discussed only the income tax implications. Unfortunately, it isn't all that simple. There are even more taxes to consider. Major ones follow:

1. *FICA.* This tax, known as self-employment tax when it isn't specifically a payroll tax, is 15.3 percent on all net business income, up to the current limit on Social Security ($87,900 in 2004) and 2.9 percent after that. This tax is only applicable for trade or business income earned either in your own name or in a business structure that doesn't protect against the tax.

2. *Alternative minimum tax.* Even the best tax planning won't necessarily protect you against the alternative minimum tax. This tax was developed years ago to ensure that the wealthiest Americans didn't completely escape paying tax. Unfortunately, many Americans making more than $50,000 are now becoming subject to this alternative method for calculating tax. Certain "tax preference" items are not allowed for alternative minimum tax calculations, and most of these items specifically target real estate professionals. To determine whether or not you are subject to paying alternative minimum tax, you must first complete a complicated form to determine the amount of alternative minimum tax due, complete your regular tax return to see how much you would pay in regular taxes, and then pay the higher of the two. Chapter 8 "Avoiding the Ticking Tax Bomb" gives some tax loopholes for the alternative minimum tax.

3. *Property tax.* The National Taxpayers Union (NTU) recently stated that it estimates 40 percent of all property owners are paying too much in property tax. Property tax is a multiple of the property tax rate times the estimated market value of

your home. In some cases the market value is additionally reduced by an assessment ratio. Whatever the assessment ratio in your area might be, the estimated market value of your house might very well be too high. Yet fewer than 5 percent of homeowners ever challenge their assessments. Governments have no incentive to change their current method of assessing. By the way, according to NTU, more than half of those who appeal their current assessments win.

4. *Transfer tax.* Real estate transactions often require payment of a transfer tax. The amount will vary based on the location of the property. For example, in Washoe County, Nevada (Reno, NV), a transfer tax equal to 0.41 percent of the gross sales price is applicable. This high cost helps the state recoup some of the tax money it has lost as gaming has grown in other states.

5. *Estate tax.* Real estate ownership is often the biggest asset that someone will have when they pass away. And depending on the value of that asset (along with other assets such as cash, personal property, and life insurance proceeds) and the year in which the person dies, there could be a lot of tax associated with the property.

STATE TAX

Besides the preceding taxes, there is also the issue of state income tax. You will pay state income tax depending on the state in which your property is located.

If you live in Arizona and own property in California, you'll pay California income tax on the California income. If you live in California and form a Nevada business structure to hold your New York property, you'll pay New York tax. There is a calculation made on your own home state tax return that will, in effect, give you some credit for the tax you pay in the other state. It isn't necessarily a dollar for dollar credit, though. The final result will depend on how the involved states calculate their taxes.

There are many opportunities for tax loopholes for real estate investors. Proactive planning helps you determine how much and when you pay your taxes.

ACTION STEPS

Income—How much cash have you generated in the past year from each of these categories?

Taxable—(earned, portfolio, passive)

Tax-deferred—(pension, Sec. 1031)

Tax-free—(ROTH, principal home, loans)

What is your current marginal tax rate?

What have you done to address alternative minimum tax and estate tax issues?

If you are paying too much in tax, what strategies do you currently use to reduce your tax rates?

After review of the preceding, what two action steps do you want to take to change the amount of tax you pay?

Chapter 2

TAX TRAPS TO AVOID

IRS LABELS

What type of real estate investor does the IRS think you are? The label they give you will make a big difference when it comes to developing your tax strategy. It all starts with first determining how you make money from real estate.

WHAT TYPE OF REAL ESTATE INVESTOR ARE YOU?

Public interest in real estate investing, just like stock investing, follows trends. Right now real estate investing is popular and the "how to" books abound. Many methods to make money are being touted, such as:

Buying foreclosures (seller predicament).

Buying "no money down" (a buying technique).

Apartment houses (type of real estate).

Commercial (type of real estate).

Trailer parks (type of real estate).

"Flips" (technique for making money—not creating cash flow).

Wholesaling (technique for making money—not creating cash flow).

Lease options (hybrid technique for creating cash flow with later sale).

Fix-up (way to create a job).

Most books show ways to find property or techniques for buying, becoming self-employed, or creating cash flow. These are all examples of plans that use real estate to achieve personal goals.

It is possible to wear more than one hat with the IRS. As we go through the three key definitions of dealer, developer, and professional, look for ways that you might be considered one of these.

DEALER, DEVELOPER, PROFESSIONAL

Of the three IRS labels for real estate investors—dealer, developer, and professional—one is fantastic and two require a little special planning. The real estate *dealer* is a designation that is assessed according to each property. It is possible to have a real estate dealer designation on one property and yet be called a real estate investor on another property.

The real estate *developer* designation is also given on a per-property basis. However, depending on how a business structure is set up, the unfavorable tax treatment meted out to a developer could impact investment properties.

The final designation, real estate *professional*, is a very desirable status. Once you or your spouse are considered a real estate professional for the year, then the benefits flow through to all properties you are actively involved with.

REAL ESTATE DEALER

A real estate dealer is someone whom the IRS considers to be involved in the "trade or business" of real estate. A real estate dealer is not a real estate investor. The designation is given property-by-property, based on what your intent toward that property actually is. If you buy a property for a quick sale, you might be considered a real estate dealer. If you buy a property and rehab it, you also might be considered a real estate dealer.

How Does the IRS Determine Real Estate Dealer Status?

There are 15 items that the IRS considers when determining real estate dealer status. The characterization of gain or loss on the sale or exchange of real property turns on whether the property was held "primarily" for sale or investment. If the IRS determines you are a dealer, then your real estate income is considered self-employed income. That means you pay self-employment tax on the net income from your business and/or real estate dealer activities.

The 15 items are:

1. Taxpayer's purpose for acquiring, holding, and selling the property.
2. Number, frequency, and continuity of sales.

3. Duration of ownership.

4. Time and effort expended by the taxpayer in promoting sales.

5. Taxpayer's use of brokers.

6. Extent of improvements and subdivision made to facilitate sales.

7. Ordinary business of the taxpayer.

8. Extent and value of the taxpayer's real estate holdings.

9. Extent and nature of the transactions involved.

10. Amount of income from sales compared with the taxpayer's other sources of income.

11. Taxpayer's desire to liquidate landholdings unexpectedly obtained.

12. Taxpayer's overall reluctance to sell the property.

13. Amount of advertising.

14. Use of a business office for sales.

15. Taxpayer's control over any sales representatives.

Of these, the most important issue appears to be the number, frequency, and continuity of sales. In other words, if you sell a lot of property, you might be considered a dealer and thus subject to taxation as a self-employed individual. One of the things the IRS will look for when attempting to provide dealer status is sales activities that show the property was held primarily for sale. These activities would include advertising, FOR SALE signs, a sales office, and employment of sales personnel.

What's Your Best Defense If You Are Classified as a Real Estate Dealer?

If your real estate activities are likely to make you a real estate dealer, then consider operating your business through an S corporation, a C corporation or a limited liability company taxed as an S corporation or a C corporation. These business structures aren't required to pay self-employment tax (they have other taxes, but generally speaking these other taxes are lower than self-employment tax). Another possible structure for real estate dealers is a limited partnership. In a limited partnership, only the general partner will be subject to self-employment tax. These structures are generally desirable for a real estate dealer to use for their quick flip properties (i.e., purchasing and selling quickly).

Review the type of structure you use to hold the property that you flip. If you have some property that is truly investment property, hold that property in a separate business structure.

While a business structure can offset the self-employment tax problem, there is one more problem that is not so easily solved. If you are a real estate dealer and you sell a quick flip property on a note that you carry back (the buyer continues to make payments to you over time), you will be responsible for paying tax immediately on all the gain. That means you could have tax due before you collect the money.

Alternatively, if you instead sell the property using the creative real estate technique of rent to own (formerly known as a "lease option"), you can initially create a rental situation that has the option of becoming a sale. You have now been able to avoid real estate dealer status by creating a rental first. Then, when your tenant/buyer exercises the right to purchase the property later, you can safely have a sale that is not subject to real estate dealer status.

Another technique to avoid being characterized as a dealer is to prove that your initial purpose for the property was to actually rent it. You can demonstrate that if you can show that you first offered up the property for rent and then later changed your mind to sell it.

Real Estate Dealer Warning

If you flip property, you might be considered a real estate dealer. Take the Real Estate Professional Status Determination Test (shown later in this chapter) to find out.

If you are a dealer:

- Hold real estate flips in a separate business structure from your real estate investment property.
- Use S corporations, C corporations, limited liability companies taxed as S corporations, or a limited partnership where another entity is the general partner.
- Do not sell property by carrying back a note.

Or you could simply not sell the property on a note that you carry back if it's a quick flip (purchase and quick sale). Sell it for cash or rent it out before you sell.

REAL ESTATE DEVELOPER TAX ISSUES

Being a real estate dealer also comes with certain tax issues that aren't always apparent. Say, for example, you find a great piece of land and decide to subdivide and develop it. Or, as a client of ours did, determine that it would make a fantastic mobile home park in an area that desperately needed affordable housing and had the proper zoning. In this case, the client did stumble on a gold mine but almost didn't survive financially because of the tax issues.

Real Estate Developer by Mistake

Bob and Ruth had found 20 acres with zoning that could easily be changed into that of a mobile home park. The 20 acres would translate into 60 spaces that would rent quickly for an average rent of $200 per month. That meant a gross income of $12,000 per month. There would be some maintenance, landscaping, and management costs. At the very high end these costs would be $3,000 per month. One of the spaces would be provided to an on-site manager, reducing the gross income by $200. They were looking at potential income of:

Gross rent	$11,800
Vacancy costs	(1,800)
Maintenance costs	(3,000)
Monthly gross	$ 7,000

The cost of the property was $200,000 and the owner would carry a note at 8 percent with 20 percent down. They estimated the improvements would cost $10,000/space and they had gotten tentative approval for a construction loan with 30 percent down. Bob and Ruth had the necessary $40,000 for the down payment for the purchase and felt they could liquidate some other resources (i.e., sell some stocks) to obtain the $180,000 they needed for their portion of the construction loan.

They had always heard that real estate provided "paper" losses that could offset their other income and so weren't

(Continued)

Real Estate Developer by Mistake *(Continued)*

worried about the tax consequences of selling their stock. After all, they reasoned, they were spending the money on another business venture.

At tax time, though, they discovered the tax truth of what they had done. The land was not depreciable. That meant that the $200,000 ($40,000 of it in cash) was all booked as an asset with no expense to offset it. The construction was considered land improvements and would be expensed or depreciated once it was completed. So at the end of the first tax year they:

- Were three-quarters of the way to completion with the project.
- Had liquidated stock, which incurred capital gains tax, and had drained all of their resources to develop the property.
- Had spent $220,000.

And none of it was a write-off. That was because Bob and Ruth were found by the IRS to be developers—much like someone building an apartment house—and none of their investment would be depreciated until it was put in service.

Bob and Ruth also discovered that the interest they had paid on the land note and for the construction project was also capitalized with the asset. The interest was not currently deductible and would instead be amortized and expensed over time. The money was flowing out, they were investing in a business, and none of it was deductible . . . yet. They had a horrible tax surprise the first year.

You are a developer if you buy a property and then do work before you put it in service. This could be true if you buy vacant land and then develop it, as in the preceding tax story. It would also be true if you bought a home and fixed it up before you rented. You would be treated as a developer during the time that you held the property before it was put in service. During this time you would not be able to take the depreciation deduction.

Uniform Capitalization Rules

Another tax issue that affects real estate developers is something called Uniform Capitalization rules. This area is a very complicated and little-understood part of tax law. Basically, if you are found to be a real estate developer, you will be forced to capitalize certain percentages (up to 100 percent!) of almost all general and administrative expenses. That means you might not only have to wait to depreciate the property but also have to capitalize all carrying expenses PLUS the general and administrative costs, such as office rent, car leases, and all the other expenses that go into making your business work. Beware of the real estate developer status!

On the opposite page is an example of how a real estate investor ventured into developer status and the disastrous tax consequences that then occurred.

CAPITALIZATION RULES The IRS considers real estate developers to be in the business of producing an inventory. In this case, that inventory may be subdivided lots, homes built for speculative purposes ("spec homes"), or even an apartment building being converted into condominiums.

The accounting will be the same as if you were operating a large manufacturing plant. You have an inventory that is being

Developer? Who, Me?

Tom and Cecilia had a successful real estate investment and property management enterprise. They had a staff of four people who helped them with the ongoing maintenance and bookkeeping for their investments. They wanted to keep growing their business but had reached a point where they simply couldn't find the deals they wanted on more real estate investments. So they decided to build new properties.

Tom had a contractor's license and they already had the beginning of a staff to work with the subcontractors he needed.

They bought their first parcel and began construction on a large, multiunit apartment house. At tax time, though, they discovered that they couldn't take a deduction for any of the payments on the land, the down payment, or the out-of-pocket expenses for construction. But they also discovered even worse news. A large portion of the administrative and salaries for their employees were now no longer deductible.

The construction of the apartment building made Tom and Cecilia now subject to Uniform Capitalization on all of their administrative expenses, even those that used to be deductible through the rest of their real estate investment business.

That first year, Tom and Cecilia had to pay an additional $15,000 in taxes. This was on top of all the out-of-pocket expenses that they had incurred during the construction of their building. Once the building was put in service, they could begin to depreciate the property. But until then the Uniform Capitalization rules became a major problem for their tax planning.

produced. That means that you must capitalize certain direct and indirect costs. Simply stated, capitalization of expenses means that you've paid money for a cost and can't take the deduction. Many new developers struggle, and some even lose their business, as they incur huge amounts of debt paying for the development costs, and yet are not able to deduct any of them. So at the end of the year they have a huge tax bill . . . and no money with which to pay it. That's the problem with capitalization.

The capitalization of direct costs, although painful when it comes to tax time, is at least more straightforward and easier to understand than the rules regarding indirect costs.

Direct Costs

Direct costs are the material and labor costs that are directly attributable to the property being developed. For example, if you develop a parcel of land to create separate subdividable lots, then you will have the costs of surveying, permits, excavation, engineering, sidewalks, and so forth. Those are direct costs related to the project. If you weren't developing the project, you wouldn't have the costs.

Direct labor used in the development process must also be capitalized. Direct labor includes full-time and part-time employees, contract employees, and independent contractors. Direct labor costs include all elements of compensation, such as overtime and vacation pay, holiday pay, and sick leave as well as regular wage amounts.

Direct costs must be added to the basis of the inventory. They are not depreciated or otherwise expensed. Instead they become part of the basis when that inventory is sold or put into productive use.

You must also capitalize the interest expense and property tax expense during the development of the project. These are also considered direct costs.

Indirect Costs

Now it gets tricky. Under the Uniform Capitalization rules of the IRS Code, you must also capitalize a "properly allocable share" of certain indirect costs.

To determine the capitalizable costs, you must allocate (or apportion) costs to the various activities of your business. For example, you would separate the development portion from the rental portion. It is generally easiest to do this by having separate business structures for these activities. It also will provide better asset protection. Along with the unfavorable tax treatment, a developer also has significant risk.

Indirect costs are all costs other than direct material costs and direct labor costs (in the case of property produced) or acquisition costs (in the case of property acquired for resale). Some examples of indirect costs include:

Indirect labor costs.

Officers' compensation.

Pension and other related costs.

Employee benefit expenses.

Indirect material costs.

Purchasing costs.

Handling costs.

Storage costs.

Cost recovery.

Depletion.

Rent.

Taxes.

Insurance.

Utilities.

Repairs and maintenance.

Engineering and design costs.

Spoilage.

Tools and equipment.

Quality control.

Bidding costs.

Licensing and franchise costs.

Capitalizable service costs.

Did you see the last one? We have yet another definition to learn if you're going to become a developer—capitalizable service costs.

Capitalizable Service Costs

Service costs are defined as a type of indirect cost (general and administrative costs) that can be identified specifically with a service department or function or that directly benefit a service department or function. For example, service departments include personnel, data processing, security, legal, and other similar departments. The determination of whether a department is a service department is based on the facts and circumstances of the taxpayer's activities and business organization.

The IRS breaks service costs into three categories: capitalizable, deductible, and mixed-use:

1. *Capitalizable service costs* are defined as service costs that directly benefit or are incurred by reason of the performance of the production or resale activities of the taxpayer. Examples of capitalizable service costs include:

   - Administration and coordination of production or resale activities (wherever performed in the taxpayer's business organization).
   - Personnel operations, including the cost of recruiting, hiring, relocating, assigning, and maintaining personnel records of employees.
   - Purchasing operations.
   - Materials handling, warehousing, and storage operations.
   - Accounting and data service operations.
   - Data processing.
   - Security services.
   - Legal services.

2. *Deductible service costs* are defined as service costs that do not directly benefit or are not incurred by reason of the performance of the production or resale activities of the taxpayer and, therefore, do not have to be capitalized. These are the expenses that you can immediately deduct. Deductible service costs generally include costs incurred by reason of the taxpayer's overall management or policy guidance functions.

   Deductible service costs also include costs incurred by reason of the taxpayer's marketing, selling, advertising, and distribution activities, and, most importantly, do not need to be capitalized.

Make a note of these. We'll come back to these costs when we talk about possible loopholes to the Uniform Capitalization rules.

3. *Mixed-service costs* are defined as service costs that are partially allocable to production or resale activities (capitalizable mixed-service costs) and partially allocable to nonproduction or nonresale activities (deductible mixed-service costs). For example, a personnel department may incur costs to develop property and it may incur costs to handle rental properties.

Real Estate Developer Good News and Bad News

If you develop real estate, you're a real estate developer. Let's start with the bad news. You must capitalize (and not immediately take a deduction for):

- Interest.
- Property tax.
- Direct costs for the project (construction, etc.).
- Capitalizable service costs.
- A portion of mixed-service costs.

The good news: You can avoid the Uniform Capitalization rules for:

- Marketing.
- Selling.
- Advertising.
- Distribution activities.

After you have identified your expenses as direct and indirect, you must then do an allocation of the costs based on the inventory held at the end of the year.

Based on this review, you might now decide to hire a CPA to make that calculation for you. We strongly recommend, though, that you and/or your bookkeeper understand the definitions of what is exempt. Set up your bookkeeping to take the best advantage of what could be a poor tax situation. Review the definitions of deductible service costs. Clarify job descriptions so that the work performed, as much as possible, becomes deductible, not capitalized. And, above all, make sure your CPA has experience in this area of accounting. It's tricky and not always well-known.

REAL ESTATE PROFESSIONAL STATUS

Now let's cover one of the good definitions! One of the biggest benefits to investing in real estate is the ability to offset the real estate paper losses (primarily caused by depreciation) against your other income. If you can qualify as a real estate professional, then 100 percent of your real estate losses can be used to offset your other income. Otherwise, this real estate paper loss is limited to $25,000 if your income is less than $100,000, and begins to phase out as your income increases. At $150,000, the $25,000 real estate paper loss is totally disallowed. But that doesn't mean the loss actually goes away. Instead, it is "suspended," to be allowed again at the time when the property sells.

One way around the paper loss limitation is if you or your spouse (if filing jointly) can qualify as a real estate professional.

Real estate professional status is based on meeting a set number of hours per year (750 hours, to be exact) that are performed in real estate functions, and, if you do other work as well, making sure that you spend more time in real estate activities than in any other activity for which you are compensated (but you still must meet the 750 hour minimum).

If you are in a real estate activity type of profession, such as a real estate agent, then you can also qualify as a real estate professional, as long as you own 5 percent or more of the business that is paying you. Don't get confused, though. As a real estate agent you are likely paid as an independent contractor, and you may even operate through your own wholly owned business structure. That's not the 5 percent we mean—we mean that you need to own 5 percent of the real estate agency you work through.

A checklist at the end of this chapter will walk you through the Real Estate Status Determination Test. Before taking it though, make sure you understand what "qualified real estate activities" are.

Qualified Real Estate Activity

A *qualified real estate activity* is any activity in which you "develop, redevelop, construct, reconstruct, acquire, convert, rent, operate, manage, lease or sell" real estate.

Remember that the key is that you perform personal services in these activities, but you don't necessarily have to be the one performing the work. You can be supervising, meeting, planning—all the activities that go into truly running a business.

- *Develop.* This includes meeting with engineers, architects, planners, equipment operators, construction personnel, drafters, financial professionals, accounting, and legal professionals, and so on, to discuss and implement development of property. You could also be involved in actually

37

performing some of the development work yourself, if you have such skills, or it could be time you spend hiring, supervising, and reviewing the work of other professionals. This development could be anything from subdividing property, with no additional amenities added, to actual construction of real property.

- *Redevelop.* This includes meeting with engineers, architects, planners, equipment operators, construction personnel, drafters, financial professionals, accounting and legal professionals, and so on, to discuss and implement demolition of structures and/or redevelopment of the property. Again, you could be involved in actually performing some of the development work yourself, if you have such skills, or it could be time you spend hiring professionals, supervising their work, reviewing plans and/or inspecting the work.

- *Construct.* As before, any meetings, planning, hiring, firing, supervision, or inspection of any phase of construction is considered performing this activity.

- *Reconstruct.* Just as with "construct," qualified activities under "reconstruct" are any ones that are necessary to this phase of building.

- *Acquire.* Acquiring a property has many phases—meeting with salespeople, looking at a whole range of properties, preparing an offering, responding to counteroffers, arranging financing, meeting with insurance agents, inspections, and actually closing a property. You don't need to acquire a property to rack up a lot of hours in this area. Don't forget to count the time you spend traveling back and forth to the property.

- *Convert.* Conversion of property is similar to redevelopment or reconstruction but might have the additional time element of meeting with planning officials. All of that time counts toward time spent in qualified real estate activities.

- *Rent.* The time spent meeting with your property managers to establish rental criteria, as well as acting as renting agent yourself (including the showing, screening, advertising, etc.), will count as qualified real estate time.
- *Operate.* If you spend time as a property manager, or meet with your property manager, then you will spend significant time as the "operator" of real estate.
- *Manage.* Similar to "operation" of real estate, if you manage your property, its tenants, prospective buyers, and so on, then you are involved in qualified real estate activity.
- *Lease.* The time spent meeting with your property managers to establish leasing criteria, as well as acting as renting agent yourself (including the showing, screening, advertising, etc.), will count as qualified real estate time.
- *Sell.* All the activities involved in selling a property (getting ready for sale, setting up open houses, placing ads, meeting with real estate brokers and prospective buyers) count toward qualified real estate time.

Real Estate Professional Status Backup

Real estate professional status is a great benefit to real estate investors as it allows you to offset your real estate paper losses against your other income. But because of its desirability it is also prone to abuse, and so the IRS has made sure that there are recordkeeping requirements to be met as well.

As we said earlier, you must spend at least 750 hours per year on real estate activities, and this must be more than the number of hours you spent on other compensated work. So if you have a job or business outside real estate, you will need to track the hours at your job or business in addition to the real estate activities. Keep a paper copy of your real estate professional time logs with your files for the year.

Real Estate Professional Tax Return Warning

You must make notice of your real estate professional status on your tax return by properly completing the tax form. Recently, we met a lady whose previous tax preparer had failed to make the proper election on her three previous tax returns. Unfortunately, her return had been picked for audit and the auditor had picked up the omitted lines. She couldn't go back and make the change. She had to add back the deductions from the real estate loss and pay the tax.

This woman had used a professional tax preparer to prepare her return, but he was not familiar with real estate taxation and so had missed this very necessary step. The lesson? Make sure your advisors really understand your business and the applicable tax strategies.

To be really sure that the IRS has been given plenty of notice that you or your spouse is a real estate professional, include a statement on your return such as:

In accordance with Section 1.146-9(g)(3), the taxpayer hereby states that he (or she) is a qualifying real estate professional under IRC Section 469(c)(7), and elects under IRC Section 469(c)(7)(A) to treat all interests in real estate as a single rental real estate activity.

ACTION STEPS

1. Take the Real Estate Professional Status Determination Test. Are there any possible issues that you need to research further or discuss with your advisor?

2. If you discover that you will be a real estate dealer on one or more properties, ensure that your business structure will eliminate self-employment tax and make sure that your exit strategy does not include selling the property over time. What changes do you need to make to protect against the real estate dealer definition?

3. If you discover that you will be considered a real estate developer on one or more properties, review the uniform capitalization issue for your service costs. Can you redefine or otherwise legally recategorize some expenses to reduce the impact of the real estate dealer status? Can you put the property in service first so that it will not be necessary to capitalize expenses at all? What changes do you need to make to protect against the real estate dealer definition?

4. Can you or your spouse be considered a real estate professional? If you currently have losses that can not be taken on your tax return, how much more time would you need to spend to qualify? Does it make sense to change circumstances to maximize the tax benefit?

5. Based on your review of the Real Estate Professional Status Determination Test, what further action steps do you need to take?

REAL ESTATE STATUS DETERMINATION TEST

Dealer/Developer/Investor

This three-part questionnaire should be completed for each individual property. The status (real estate dealer/developer/investor) is determined on a property-by-property basis. Generally, the client will want the investor status on property, as it avoids the self-employment tax, and does not accelerate tax due on properties sold with a note of the dealer and avoids the uniform capitalization requirements of the developer.

---

1. What was the intent when the property was purchased?

   *If the answer is that it was to be rented or otherwise held as a long-term investment, then **ask the next question;** otherwise **go to 2.***

   How long was the property held before it was sold?

   *If property is still owned, or was held for at least a year prior to sale, this will generally qualify as a real estate investment. **Go on to the next property.***

   *If the property is to be extensively rehabilitated, demolished, or developed prior to use or sale, **go to 3.***

   *If the property was sold (even if that sale was done with a land sale contract, seller financing, or other form of carried-back note) after being held less than one year, **go to 2.***

2. If the property was sold within one year, do you have evidence that the sale was as a result of a change of plans?

   A change of plans means that the owner started out with one intent and then later changed that intent. Typically, you will want to

---

show proof that an early sale was a change of plans; otherwise, you will have Real Estate Dealer status.

A change of plans could be shown as a result of other financial issues of the owner—change in marital status, move, change in income, other expenses, or as a result of trying to rent it and being unsuccessful.

If evidence can be shown that the sale was done as a result of a change of plans, then this property qualifies as a real estate investment. Note that the gain would be subject to the short-term capital gains rate, not the long-term capital gains rate. **Go on to the next property.**

If the property is shown to have been sold with the initial intent at the time of purchase to sell, then the property will qualify as under the dealer status. **Go on to the next property.**

3. If the property was purchased with the intent of extensive remodeling or rehabilitation, was the property first put in service as a real estate investment property?

If the property was initially rented in the same purpose as the ultimate use, such as by renting out half of the units in an apartment building while you extensively remodel the other half, then you have an investment property with remodeling costs. The property should be depreciated, and the current expenses such as mortgage interest and property tax can be expensed. **Go to the next property.**

If the property had a use that wasn't the same as the development purpose, such as the rental as pasture for part of the land while a trailer park was being constructed, the property might still be subject to Uniform Capitalization. Review the magnitude of the development costs in relationship to the rental of the property and determine reasonableness of status. **Go to the next property.**

If the property was bought solely to be renovated, this property will be a developer property. **Go to the next property.**

Real Estate Professional

Real estate professional status is unrelated to the issue of dealer, developer, or investor status of the property. This test is strictly a test of hours spent in real estate activities. Review the real estate activities list prior to completion of the following four questions.

1. Are you employed by a company that is engaged in real estate activity? If so, do you own 5 percent or more of that company?

   *If the answer is yes, **you are a Real Estate Professional**. If the answer is no, **continue with 2**.*

2. Do you work outside the home?

   *If the answer is no, then **go to 4**. If the answer is yes, **go to 3**.*

3. Do you spend more hours in real estate activities on an annual basis than you do in your other business?

   *If the answer is no, then **you cannot qualify as a Real Estate Professional**. If you're married and file a joint return, have your spouse complete this portion of the questionnaire. If the answer is yes, then **go to 4**.*

4. Do you spend a minimum of 750 hours per year in real estate activities?

   *If you answered yes and have no other profession, **you are a Real Estate Professional**. If you answered yes and passed the test in question 3, **you are a Real Estate Professional**. If you answered no, **you cannot be a Real Estate Professional**.*

PART II

Real Estate Loopholes

Chapter 3

TURNING A LOSS INTO AN ASSET

REAL ESTATE LOSS

Most of us hate to lose; yet when it comes to real estate loopholes, losing can be the best thing that ever happened to you. That's because the right kind of loss can create tax benefits. And if the loss didn't cost you any cash, you've just received a huge tax gift. First, though, let's review the different types of losses that can occur with real estate. There are actually four different types of losses that can occur:

1. Real losses.
2. Loss from sale.
3. Suspended loss.
4. Paper loss.

Real Losses

We use the term *real loss* to identify the actual cost of owning a property that does not provide sufficient rental income to cover the ongoing expenses. The real loss means it costs you real cash on an ongoing basis. Investors in highly appreciating areas often experience the gap that occurs between the purchase price of a property (which increases over time through appreciation) and the rental value (which increases with inflation). The rental income simply hasn't kept up with the purchase price, and cash flow is negative.

Real losses cost you real money and, unfortunately, depending on how much money you make and how you much you participate in this activity and in other real estate activities, you may not be able to take full advantage of the loss against your other income.

A real loss can be a serious problem if you haven't properly prepared for the loss on your tax return.

LOSS FROM SALE

When you sell property (or any other type of asset), you will experience a gain or a loss in one of three tax categories:

1. Ordinary gain or loss.
2. Capital gain or loss.
3. Hybrid gain or loss.

Ordinary Gain or Loss

An *ordinary gain or loss* comes about when you sell property that is held primarily for sale to customers as part of your regular business activities. It is similar to inventory, in that it has been purchased for resale, not use. For a real estate investor, selling a piece of property for which you are considered a real estate dealer means that you will have an ordinary gain or loss.

These gains and losses cannot be used to offset against capital gains or losses.

Capital Gain or Loss

The sale of a capital asset creates *a capital gain or loss*. Capital assets include all property, regardless of how long held, with the following exceptions:

- Inventory from a taxpayer's business.
- Property held by a taxpayer primarily for sale to customers.
- Depreciable property used in a trade or business.
- Real property used in a trade or business.

Real estate that has been depreciated is not a capital asset under this definition. Real estate that has not been used in a trade or business, such as a piece of land, a vacation home, or a portion of your gain in excess of the tax-free gain exclusion, is considered a capital asset. A capital loss is limited to $3,000 plus the amount of current capital gains. The rest of the capital loss must be carried forward to subsequent years. Unfortunately, a homeowner who sees their house go down in value is generally stuck with a capital loss that cannot be used.

The current favorable capital gains rate occurs when a property is sold after it has been held for more than one year. Otherwise the short-term capital gains rate, which is the same as the ordinary income tax rate, is applicable.

Hybrid Gain or Loss

If you have real estate that has been depreciated, it is considered Section 1231 property. This *hybrid* form of taxation is actually

---

Before You Sell

Before you sell any property:

- Estimate amount of the gain or loss.
- Determine character of the gain.
- Ordinary gain/loss = subject to ordinary income tax rates + self-employment tax.
- Capital gain/loss = if held more than one year, capital gains rates, can be used to offset other capital gains/losses.
- Hybrid gain/loss = if gain, treated as capital gain; if loss, treated as ordinary loss.

---

the best of all worlds. If the property is sold for a profit and has been held for more than a year, it will receive long-term capital gains benefits. If the property is sold for a loss, it is treated as an ordinary loss. An ordinary loss can then be used to offset ordinary income.

Property Sold inside a Business Structure

If you had held your real estate within a business structure (commonly a limited liability company, limited partnership, or occasionally an S corporation), the gain would all flow through to the individual owners, who are then taxed based on the character of the gain when the entity sold it. In other words, if a property is sold that is owned by a limited liability company and that property created a hybrid loss, the hybrid loss will flow through to the individual owners of the limited liability company.

Suspended Loss

If you have a real estate loss during the regular operation of a property, you will have to pass some tests in order to take the loss against other income. First, you will need to prove that you materially participated in the activity of running that property. If you haven't materially participated, none of the loss will be allowed. Even after you've passed that test, you'll be able to deduct only $25,000 of the loss against your income if you make less than $100,000, phasing out to nothing at all if you make more than $150,000. The only way around this loss limitation is to qualify as a real estate professional, as we discussed earlier.

If you have a loss in excess of what is allowed in a particular year, or if your income is too high and you lose the loss deductible entirely, that loss will be suspended until the property is sold. In the year that the property is sold, the suspended losses are fully allowed against all forms of income.

Paper Loss

Finally, we come to the type of loss that makes real estate investors rich—a paper loss. A *paper loss* is a legal loss that occurs for a property even though there is actually a positive cash flow from the property. The secret is a phantom expense called depreciation.

The government allows you to take a deduction each year for *depreciation*, which is the amount they tell you that your property has gone down in value. The theory of depreciation is that real or personal property gradually degrades over time. In the case of personal property, such as vehicles, this theory is true. Anyone who has ever purchased a car and has immediately seen the value decrease can attest to the validity of depreciation for personal property. But real property is another story. Does it really go down in value? In some areas yes, but generally over time real property appreciates. It goes up in value.

This is an example of a loophole that Congress has provided for real estate investors. Even though we know that property, if bought right and maintained to its fullest potential, will go up dramatically in value, Congress lets us take a deduction for a reduction in value. The IRS provides tables to calculate how much the depreciation will be for your property.

Classes of Property

First, you will need to classify the "class" of the property involved with your investment. This is a very critical process that, unfortunately, most investors and their accountants only partially complete. Here are the four steps (five, for California and some other states!):

1. Break out the value of the land separately from the structure. Land is not depreciable. Here's a tip: Many times the value of a bare lot in the area plus the cost of the construction does not equal the total purchase price. The professionals compare the assessor's statement of value for the land and building with the purchase price. Use the same ratio that the assessor used for land to building against the total price for your property to determine the value ratio between land and building.

2. Break out the value of personal property items (chattels) within your building. The best way to do this is to have an appraiser help you with the value of these items, or check out ChattelAppraisals.com for help in determining

the value of all personal property items. If you can't find an appraiser in your area, use the fair market value (FMV) of the personal property items, and then compare that value with the total cost of the building. Generally, it's hard to substantiate more than 30–40 percent of total building value in personal property items. Personal property items are depreciated over a shorter lifespan, typically ranging from 7 to 15 years.

3. The value of the structure is the total price less land less personal property. This is then depreciated as real property. Currently, real property used for residential rental purposes is depreciated over 27.5 years, and real property used for commercial purposes is depreciated over 39 years. If a property was placed in service prior to May 13, 1993, it will have different depreciation lives.

4. The depreciation for real and personal property is then subtracted from your operating income for the property. (*Operating income* means that you have deducted the costs of the property, such as mortgage interest, property tax, insurance, homeowner's dues, utilities, and repairs as well as your business expenses).

5. In some states, such as California, you are also required to keep depreciation schedules using the state's assignment of life. This is where you really need to have a good tax software program. Otherwise, you are going to compile a lot of spreadsheets!

How to Catch Up Past Accelerated Depreciation

The step that many taxpayers miss is #2, because they forget to take out the value of personal property. Internal estimates at

Diane's office, based on a review of their clients' past records, indicate that more than 90 percent of those returns had made this very common mistake. This mistake cost those taxpayers thousands of dollars each!

However, if you have made this common mistake in the past, don't despair. You can recover the past depreciation with your next tax return by filing a Form 3115 and attaching a statement.

What Happens When You Sell?

When you sell your property, you will be required to recapture the depreciation at ordinary income tax rates. You then pay the capital gains rate on the difference between the basis and the sales price (less costs). Or you can delay the tax through a like-kind exchange.

Common Depreciation Mistake

Another common mistake has much more potentially damaging consequences. Some taxpayers have made the mistake of not deducting depreciation on their investment property. If you've made this mistake, correct it immediately by filing to take the past depreciation with your current tax return. The IRS is going to assume you took it when you sold, and will recapture the depreciation that was previously taken (or that could have been taken), when you calculate your gain. You'll have to pay tax on that recaptured depreciation even if you didn't take it and there's nothing to recapture!

Plan Your Losses

Prior to year end, determine the following for each property:

- What, if any, operating "real" loss will there be?
- What, if any, paper loss is there after current depreciation?
- If you are able to take a real estate loss, is there more depreciation that you can take?
- If you have a loss that can't be taken, can you create income to offset it?
- If you still have a loss that can't be taken, can you or your spouse qualify as a real estate professional?

MULTIPLE PROPERTIES

If you have more than one property, you have an option as to whether you want to combine your activities on each property, for tax report purposes. If you don't combine activities, you will have to pass the material participation test for each individual property.

This is a separate test from the real estate professional test in the previous chapter. Even if you are a real estate professional, if you do not materially participate in the property, you will not be able to take a deduction for any of the loss, no matter how much the loss is or how much your income is.

As you are determining whether you want to aggregate activities, make sure that the activity really is a rental, and secondly determine whether you have materially participated in one or more of them.

Multiple Properties
Could Mean Multiple Headaches

Sandra is a single mom who balanced raising her young daughter with a full-time job and still found time to buy five single-family homes. She had seen the properties go up in value and had refinanced three of them to take out the money to buy the other two. She showed a loss on three of the properties during the first year she had all five properties. But she didn't worry about it because her income was under $100,000, so she reasoned she'd be able to take full advantage of the write-offs.

Sandra knew that she would also need to prove that she had spent 500 hours during the year on the properties, but she wasn't sure if that meant 500 hours per property, or 500 hours in total. With a full-time job outside the home and her full-time job single-handedly raising her daughter, there was no way that Sandra could spend 2,500 hours (500 hours times 5 properties) on active participation in the properties. And, luckily, she didn't have to! Sandra was able to successfully aggregate all the properties so that she took full advantage of the real estate loss against her other income. The aggregation of the properties on her tax return meant that she only had to prove that she materially participated for 500 hours, not 2,500 hours.

RENTAL ACTIVITY

What is a rental? The answer, like a lot of tax law, isn't so obvious. Basically, an activity is a *rental activity* if gross income received pays for the use of the property and if the activity isn't one of the exceptions. If you have an activity that meets one of the following six exceptions, you actually have a business, not a rental.

1. **Average per-tenant use is seven days or less.** Rental property that is used by each tenant for an average of less than seven days is not a rental activity. Calculate this by dividing the total number of days of actual tenant use (not days available) by the actual customer numbers (i.e., 210 days divided by 150 customers). Most vacation condominiums are considered a business because they fail this portion of the requirement for meeting the rental requirement.

2. **Average tenant use is greater than 7 days, but less than 30 days and significant personal services are provided.** If you provide significant personal services, such as maid service, registration service, and room service, you might have a business. In general, *significant* is defined as services that are provided frequently and have a value. Under this definition, any kind of longer-term bed and breakfast would be a business, not a rental.

3. **Extraordinary personal services are provided to the tenant.** If extraordinary personal services are provided to the tenant, there is a business as well. An example might be a hospital boarding house.

4. **Rental is incidental to the business activity.** The rule is actually a little more complicated. If the reason that you own a property is clearly because of the investment potential through appreciation (such as a piece of raw land) and the gross rental income is less than 2 percent of the lesser of the property's unadjusted basis or fair market value, then the property would not be considered a rental property. For example, let's say that you own a piece of raw land for

which you paid $100,000, and it is now worth $150,000. The lesser amount is $100,000. You would need to collect more than $2,000 per year in rent for the property to be considered a rental property. Otherwise the property is considered an investment. That means that the property expenses will have to be reported on a separate schedule (Schedule A—Itemized Deductions) as investment expenses and will only be allowed up to the extent of investment income. No loss would be allowed against other property.

5. **Business activity is renting to customers.** Property made available during defined business hours for the nonexclusive use of customers is not a rental activity. For example, receiving a payment for golf course greens fees is not a rental.

6. **Owner provides property to a partnership or S corporation.** If the taxpayer owns an interest in a partnership, S corporation, or a joint venture that is considered a business, and the taxpayer owns property that is rented to that business, the property is not considered a rental property.

WHAT IF YOU DON'T HAVE A RENTAL?

If you've reviewed the six preceding exceptions and discovered you don't really have a deductible rental, what now? Well, chances are you just discovered that the property you thought was a rental is actually one of the following two items:

1. It is an investment property.
2. It is a business property.

If your property is an investment property, you may be able to increase the rents to have the property meet the rental income standard. If you can't, then investment expense limitations will apply. Investment expenses include interest costs for investments (margin interest, for example) and other costs directly associated with investment properties. These are reported on your Schedule A. So your first challenge is to make sure you itemize all deductions on your tax return. If you don't, you will have a problem with taking a deduction for these expenses. Another limitation is that total investment expenses are allowed only to the extent of investment income. Investment expenses more than that amount will be carried forward to subsequent years.

If your property is a business, you will then need to consider whether you have a legitimate business that can show a loss that can be taken against other sources of income. The test for a legitimate business includes items such as:

- You carry on the activity in a businesslike manner.
- The time and effort you put into the activity indicate you intend to make it profitable.
- You depend on income from the activity for your livelihood.
- Your losses are due to circumstances beyond your control (or are normal in the startup phase of your type of business).
- You change your methods of operation in an attempt to improve profitability.
- You, or your advisors, have the knowledge needed to carry on the activity as a successful business.
- You were successful in making a profit in similar activities in the past.
- The activity makes a profit in some years (how much profit it makes is also considered).
- You can expect to make a future profit from the appreciation of the assets used in the activity.

MATERIALLY PARTICIPATE

There's one more definition to worry about when you're looking at how you can deduct your real estate losses, and that is *material participation*. What does it mean to materially participate, and why is that important?

It's important because the grouping of income and losses for passive activities (i.e., rentals and ownership in businesses) is determined first by whether those activities are actually passive (rental or passive ownership in a limited partnership or S corporation) and secondly, by whether there is material participation.

Material participation in rental activities is necessary to take any kind of deduction. Even if your income is less than $100,000 per year, you will not be able to take a rental loss against that income unless you can prove that you had material participation.

You are materially participating in an activity if you can meet one of the following tests:

- **Work 500 hours in the activity.** If you work 500 or more hours in the activity, you are considered to be materially participating. Unfortunately, you can't annualize this requirement. If you buy a rental property halfway through the year, you still must work the full 500 hours. Here's a tip: While spouses cannot combine hours to reach the real estate professional minimum of 750 hours, they can combine hours to reach the 500 hour requirement, as long as they file a joint return.
- **Do substantially all the work.** If you perform 70 percent or more of the work in the activity, you will be considered to be materially participating.
- **Work 100 hours and no one else does more.** This exception saved the day for a couple with a vacation condo. They were able to prove that they worked 100 hours leasing up

the condo and that the management condo had not spent that much time on their condo.

■ **Work 500 hours in aggregated activities.** You can claim that you have materially participated when your activities can be combined and your total participation is 500 hours or more.

■ **Materially participate for 5 of the past 10 years.** You can be considered to be materially participating in an activity if you materially participate in it for any 5 taxable years during the past 10 taxable years.

■ **Materially participate in any three previous years in a "personal service activity."** Now, this is a strange exception. There is no limit on when the three years run. But, basically, if you've ever been a real estate professional for three years, you have a "get out of jail free" card forever on meeting the material participation rules for your properties.

■ **Regular, continuous, and substantial activity.** This is one of those "and everything else" types of rules. In other words, you can't identify exactly what the IRS is looking for here, but they'll let you know if you've got it. We recommend that you keep track of all activities and if it's anything like other "regular, continuous, and substantial" types of rules (such as for active stock traders), expect the burden of proof to be on you. The IRS won't want to see long breaks in activity (i.e., you take the summer off) and will want to see consistent activity each and every week, if possible.

GROUPING ACTIVITIES

We've covered what the IRS considers a rental, what to do if your activity is considered a business or an investment, and what they want to see to prove material participation. Now let's take another look at what it takes to group activities. You will have to prove you have materially participated in each and every activity unless you group them together.

Activity grouping is an important part of your tax planning, yet the IRS does not clearly define the word *activity*. However, it does give us the five following guidelines:

1. Similarities and differences in the respective types of activities.
2. The extent of common control among activity.
3. The respective geographic locations of each activities.
4. The extent of common ownership among the activities.
5. The interdependencies among the activities.

TURNING A LOSS INTO AN ASSET

You might be asking yourself why we've had so much discussion about losses. After all, aren't you buying real estate to make money, not lose it? That's absolutely true. And one of the ways that you can make money—in fact a lot of money—is by taking advantage of the tax benefits that real estate losses can provide. In fact, if you are following the rules for material participation, properly aggregating properties on your return, and you or your spouse can qualify as a real estate professional, you shouldn't have to pay taxes. If all of the above are true and you do pay taxes, then one of two things is happening: (1) You don't own enough real estate, or (2) you aren't properly taking advantage of all the real estate loopholes available. A real estate paper loss is an asset when it is part of an overall tax-advantaged, wealth-building strategy.

ACTION STEPS

1. Will you have a loss from your real estate investments? If so, which kind?

2. Do you currently materially participate in your real estate activities? If not, what can you do, so that you meet this test?

3. Will you be able to take advantage of losses from your real estate? If not, what can you do to minimize the losses?

4. After reviewing the preceding, what action steps do you want to take immediately?

Chapter 4

SMART BUSINESS STRUCTURES THAT REDUCE RISK AND TAX

O ne of the problems with property is that you run a much bigger risk of loss than you do with stocks. People might sue you. We call them tenants! And if you are sued and found liable for damages to someone, all of your assets are potentially at risk of being seized and sold by a creditor to pay the judgment against you.

WHY HOLDING PROPERTY IN YOUR OWN NAME IS RISKY

With real estate, particularly rental real estate, you are ultimately responsible for what happens on the property. That means that if a tenant, or the guest of a tenant, is injured while on your property, that person has a claim against you, as the landlord, because you did not provide a safe environment. Even if you just hold vacant land, you still need to be careful. If there is a hazard on your property, say an open pit, or an unmarked hot spring, you may be held liable for injuries that occur on the property—even if the person injured was trespassing!

INSURANCE ALONE MAY NOT BE ENOUGH

Homeowners insurance is always your first line of defense, but it may not be enough by itself. If your policy lapses and you don't realize it right away, or your insurance company no longer covers that type of claim, or especially if the insurance company finds that you have done something to breach the terms of the policy, they can deny claims coverage. And if that happens, you can bet that the claimant will come looking to you to make things right.

BUSINESS STRUCTURES PROVIDE REAL ESTATE ASSET PROTECTION

Because of the risk to your personal assets we recommend that you always hold property in a legal business structure. That is because legal business structures, properly formed and maintained, act as a shield between you and your business. Even though you might own the business, the assets that you hold and the assets that the business holds are treated separately. The business structure is treated as a legal person, and this one simple fact can save you thousands in the event of a lawsuit. Before, if a tenant was injured on your property and sued you, all of your assets were at risk. On the other hand, putting your real estate into a business structure (i.e., the business structure owns the asset and you own the business), means that if that same tenant injury occurs, the tenant cannot sue you personally; he or she can sue only the business structure. While there is no question that this would impact that real estate property, it would not affect your personal assets and other real estate, as long as the other real estate is held in a separate business structure.

BUSINESS STRUCTURES PROVIDE PERSONAL ASSET PROTECTION, TOO

This works in the opposite direction, too. Say that you are responsible for an accident or owe money and are sued by a creditor. The same barrier that prevented an injured tenant from trying to seize your personal property can also be used to prevent a personal creditor from trying to seize your business structure's assets.

NOT ALL BUSINESS STRUCTURES ARE THE SAME

How much you can protect yourself and your real estate assets depends on the type of business structure that you choose to hold your real estate. Not all are ideal for holding real estate assets, either legally or, more particularly, from a tax standpoint. The IRS treats businesses differently, depending on the type of business structure. The right one can save you taxes. The wrong one can cost you thousands.

CHOOSING THE RIGHT BUSINESS STRUCTURE

Before you can choose a business structure, you need to know what your options are. Here is a review of the types of business structures available and the tax and legal considerations you need to know.

There are four business structures that you can use to hold ownership to your property. These are (1) C corporation, (2) S corporation, (3) partnership, and (4) limited liability company. Three of these structures, the S corporation, partnership, and limited liability company, have flow-through taxation, meaning tax is assessed and paid by the individual owners based on their ownership percentage. The C corporation does not have flow-through taxation and pays its own taxes.

We have prepared a vocabulary chart (see following page) that might help you to understand the structure and terminology used for different business entities. Then, after you've looked at the chart, continue reading about the qualities and failings of each of these entity structures.

C Corporation

A C corporation is not a good choice for holding real estate, from a tax perspective. This is because the capital gains rate for the corporate level is much higher than it is for other types of business structures. This is partially due to the way that a C corporation files its taxes. It does so as a separate and distinct entity, and because it does so, regular tax rates are lower, at least for the first $50,000 of income. But those lower taxes are balanced against the higher capital gains rate. So while holding a C corporation is not a problem to begin with, when you go to sell the property later, and especially if it has appreciated

Business Structure Vocabulary

	C Corporation	S Corporation	Limited Partnership	Limited Liability Company
Owners	Shareholders	Shareholders	Limited Partners	Members
Ownership Units	Shares	Shares	Limited Partnership Interests	Membership Interests
Management Structure	Directors and Officers	Directors and Officers	General Partner	Manager, or Managing Members
Management Duties	Officers carry out business operations and report to Directors, who report to Shareholders. Only officers can enter contracts and can bind corporation.	Officers carry out business operations and report to Directors, who report to Shareholders. Only officers can enter contracts and can bind corporation.	General Partner has sole control over business operations, can enter into contracts, and can bind the limited partnership.	Manager or Managing Members have control over business operations, can enter into contracts, and can bind the limited liability company.
Management liability for business debts or for actions against the structure	None, unless management commits or allows illegal actions by or on behalf of the corporation.	None, unless management commits or allows illegal actions by or on behalf of the corporation.	General Partner remains liable for debts and illegal actions of the limited partnership.	None, unless Managers or Managing Members commit or allow illegal actions by or on behalf of the LLC.
Flow-Through Taxation?	No	Yes	Yes	Yes
Tax Quirks	Profits are taxed at corporate level and then again at shareholder level, where they show up as dividends or distributions.	Medical premiums are considered a taxable benefit to shareholders owning more than 2% of the corporation. In a C corporation, owner/shareholders do not pay tax on medical benefits received.	Profits that are held for reinvestment in the limited partnership instead of being distributed still incur tax to the limited partners.	Profits that are held for reinvestment in the LLC instead of being distributed still incur tax to the members. All business income is subject to self-employment tax.
Favorable capital gains treatment for asset sales?	No	Yes (preferable to C corporations, but still not as good as LLC/LP)	Yes	Yes

(Continued)

Business Structure Vocabulary *(Continued)*

	C Corporation	S Corporation	Limited Partnership	Limited Liability Company
Availability of Tax Deductions and Loopholes	Best	Good	Better	Better
Suitability for holding real estate or other appreciating assets?	Unsuitable unless foreign residents are involved.	Can be used, but not recommended.	Very suitable	Very suitable
Creditor Protection	Owners cannot be sued for business liability. Owners may lose control of corporation shares (and assets) in a personal lawsuit.	Owners cannot be sued for business liability. Owners may lose control of corporation shares (and assets) in a personal lawsuit.	General Partner may be sued for business liability. Limited partners may not be sued. Owners cannot lose control of limited partnership interests (and assets) to creditors in a personal lawsuit unless they (1) live in a state that allows creditors to seize assets and (2) a creditor obtains a special court order allowing the seizure.	Owners cannot be sued for business liability. Owners cannot lose control of limited partnership interests (and assets) to creditors in a personal lawsuit unless they (1) live in a state that allows creditors to seize assets and (2) a creditor obtains a special court order allowing the seizure.

significantly in value, you will pay far more in taxes than you would if you held that property in the other three types of business structure.

There is also a legal problem with holding real estate in a C corporation. As the owner of the C corporation, you own shares of its stock. Those shares are legally considered to be a personal asset. That doesn't affect anything if a tenant is injured and sues the corporation as the property's owner, but it does affect things if you are sued personally by someone. The law considers shares of stock to be personal assets that may be seized and sold to pay judgments and debts, and that means a judgment creditor could argue that he or she should be able to seize your shares to help pay a judgment against you.

There is one situation where holding real estate in a C corporation might make sense, and that is where foreign ownership is involved. For tax purposes, a foreign owner is someone who does not file and pay taxes in the United States (as opposed to legal residents and immigrants who may not be U.S. citizens but do pay taxes). Foreign owners can hold interests in LLCs and limited partnerships, but this means considerably more bookkeeping and recordkeeping by the business structure. Foreign owners cannot own shares in an S corporation at all. If you do have foreign owners involved in your real estate investment plans, you may want to discuss the matter ahead of time with your advisors, to see what options are available to you that will not impact the rest of your shareholders.

S Corporation

An S corporation is a better choice than a C corporation to hold real estate, but it is still not an optimum choice.

From a tax point of view, an S corporation is an acceptable choice. It offers flow-through taxation, meaning that the profits of the S corporation flow through to all of its shareholders as "distributions," and are taxed at each shareholder's individual tax rate. Another benefit is that the earnings of an S corporation are not subject to self-employment tax (while the earnings from an LLC are). However, because passive real estate income isn't subject to self-employment tax in any event, this may not be a significant factor.

When an S corporation does distribute profits to shareholders though, those profits are distributed at "fair market value." This can be a problem, because when a piece of real estate is sold, the property must distribute out at the current fair market value. That means there is likely to be a "taxable event" as the property hopefully has appreciated as you have held it. *To distribute* means to pay tax. But, if you wait to distribute, the situation will only worsen.

Another problem with using S corporations to hold real estate is a lack of flexibility. Shareholders are entitled to receive distributions in the same percentage as their individual ownership percentage. So if you have a 70:30 ownership split between two shareholders, one will get 70 percent of the profit (and pay tax on that money), while the other shareholder will receive the other 30 percent of the profit, and pay tax on it. But if you have a situation where you have a money shareholder, and a work shareholder, that is, one shareholder puts up the down payment and renovation costs, while the other shareholder does the physical work, then you may want to pay back the money shareholder first. For example, maybe you want to pay the money shareholder 85 percent of the profits for the first three years, to pay back the renovation costs as soon as possible. You can't do this in an S corporation, because the profit split is rigidly limited to 70:30. That is not the case with LLCs, which is why they are a better choice of business structure.

The final reason to avoid using S corporations to hold real estate is that it has the same legal issue that impacts a C corporation. The owners hold shares in the S corporation, and those shares can be seized and sold by creditors, just as your other assets could be. This is not the case in LLCs and limited partnerships, which is why these latter two entities are better choices to hold real estate.

There is one situation where using an S corporation to hold

real estate does work well, and that is for *flips* (i.e., purchase and quick sales). If your real estate business consists of flipping property, then the income could be considered active trade or business and thus subject to self-employment tax. In this case, an S corporation might make more sense, because you can set up an income split, where part of the income from the S corporation flows through to shareholders as employment income, which is subject to income and payroll tax, and profit distributions, which are subject to income tax only. You can't do the income split in an LLC or a limited partnership, unless you structure your LLC in a very specific manner.

Partnership

There are two types of partnerships: the general partnership and the limited partnership. The general partnership is a bad entity and provides no legal or tax benefits for its owners. We *never* recommend using a general partnership to hold real estate. The limited partnership, on the other hand, is a tried and true entity and is one of the two best entities to hold real estate.

Limited partnership tax law is very favorable for real estate holdings. Like an S corporation, a limited partnership has flow-through taxation. Limited partnership income, including both passive rent and capital gains income, all flow through to the individual owners, and the tax is paid at individual limited partners' levels.

Another benefit of limited partnership tax law is the tremendous flexibility possible. Distributions from a limited partnership come out at "basis" rather than at fair market value the way that S corporation distributions do. This allows you to move assets in and out of a limited partnership without tax consequence. The limited partnership is also a very easy structure in which to do a Section 1031, Like-Kind Tax Deferred exchange.

Legally, a limited partnership is an excellent entity for holding real estate, especially if you are thinking about estate planning in combination with real estate investing. That is because the limited partners have only a passive role in operating the business of the limited partnership. So parents can control the business activities, even though their children may own the majority of the limited partnership. Some of the strongest limited partnership law revolves around the ability to set up and maintain this control.

Another excellent benefit to using a limited partnership is that it is much more difficult for judgment creditors to take control of a limited partnership by seizing its ownership interests. In fact, in many states it is not possible at all. Most states have adopted the Uniform Limited Partnership Act, which provides that ownership interests of a limited partnership are not subject to seizure and sale, in the way that C and S corporation shares are. So if you are sued personally, depending on what state you live in, a judgment creditor may not be able to access the assets held in your limited partnership by seizing your ownership interests. As with C and S corporations though, if the limited partnership itself is sued, the assets it holds may be at risk for seizure and sale.

There is one distinct feature that limited partnerships have that other business structures don't, and that involves liability for the general partner. In a limited partnership, there are two types of partners: the general partner, who manages the business of the limited partnership and the limited partners, who own the limited partnership but do not participate in its operation. In the other three business structures, C corporations, S corporations, and LLCs the management team is usually protected from liability for the actions and debts of the business. However, in a limited partnership, the general partner is not protected and remains liable.

Although this looks like a serious disadvantage on the face of it, it is actually quite easy to compensate for. By setting up a management-protected entity and making it the general partner instead of you personally, you can make sure that any liability will fall on the business structure, instead of you personally.

In some states, the limited partnership is the preferred entity for real estate holdings. This is usually due to that state's taxation methods. For example, in Texas and California limited partnerships pay lower fees and franchise taxes than limited liability companies. In most states, however, an LLC taxed as a limited partnership is the preferred structure.

Limited Liability Company (LLC)

LLCs are an interesting blend of corporation and limited partnership. They provide the flexible, flow-through tax advantages of a limited partnership, with the liability protection of a corporation (i.e., the managers of an LLC are not usually liable for the actions or debts of the LLC). Like a limited partnership, LLCs are largely governed in most states by the Uniform Limited Liability Company Act, which provides that ownership interests in an LLC are not necessarily subject to seizure and sale in the same fashion that C or S corporation shares are.

When it comes to taxes though, the LLC is a truly unique creature. The LLC can elect how it wants to be taxed. It can choose to be taxed like a C corporation, file its own tax return, and pay C corporation-style taxes. It can choose to be taxed as an S corporation, allowing the owners to split the income into a salary stream (subject to income and payroll taxes) and a distribution stream (subject to income tax only). An LLC can choose to be taxed like a limited partnership, with flow-through tax benefits and the ability to be flexible in how the profits are distributed. An LLC can even choose to be taxed as an individual taxpayer (we call that one a "disregarded entity," because the IRS disregards the LLC structure and taxes it as though you owned the assets directly). The disregarded entity taxation can be very useful because even though the IRS considers it "disregarded," the legal system certainly doesn't, meaning assets held in that type of LLC are as safe from creditors as any other LLC.

For holding real estate, we want the LLC to be taxed either as a limited partnership or as a disregarded entity (also called a "Schedule E" tax entity). These two methods offer the best blend of tax savings and legal protection. Even if you and your spouse own real estate together, as long as you own it jointly (i.e., you are both listed as owning 100 percent) and file a joint tax return, you can still claim disregarded entity status for your LLC.

Now, think about how this relates to your family home for just a minute. For those of you just beginning your real estate investing career, your family home is probably the most valuable asset that you own. Can you think of a good reason not to put this asset into a protected entity?

FOUR MORE REASONS TO USE AN LLC OR LP FOR REAL ESTATE INVESTING

Now that you understand a little bit about the types of business structures available, and why we suggest using an LLC or a limited partnership for holding real estate over the C and S corporations, here are four more reasons to use an LLC or limited partnership:

1. Capital gains treatment.
2. Tax benefit for flow-through passive losses.
3. Potential distribution of assets.
4. Charging order protection.

Capital Gains

You know that the LLC and the limited partnership are both flow-through entities, with the gains and losses flowing through to the individual taxpayer. Hopefully, when you sell the property in the future, you will realize a profit on the sale. But if you use a C or S corporation to hold the real estate, you will pay much more in capital gains than you would by using an LLC or a limited partnership, because corporations must report the sale at fair market value, while LLCs and limited partnerships can use the "basis" instead. Even if you cannot set off the entire capital gains with the basis, by having the profits taxed at everyone's individual tax rate, you will still lower the overall taxes paid, because capital gains rates are lower for individuals than for corporations.

Tax Benefit

An LLC or limited partnership may also flow through passive losses to its owners, particularly if the Loophole #2—Accelerated Depreciation or Loophole #3—Real Estate Professional, has been used. You want those benefits for yourself! Make sure you use one of these two flow-through entities to maximize your ability to take these loopholes.

Distributions

We have talked about the problem with S corporation distributions, in that you must use fair market value instead of "basis" value, and that you are restricted to the ownership percentages on the books when you are distributing S corporation profits. Here's another wrinkle. Say you own a large piece of property and it is subdivided. You may not have planned to have it subdivided, but say it happens anyway! In the case of one of our clients, one acre from a large piece of property was taken by the state. Because that acre was in the middle of the property, our clients now had two pieces of property left. For our clients to move one piece of property out into its own business structure, they would have to transfer the property, incur transfer taxes, AND pay capital gains tax, even though the land wasn't really changing hands to an outside third party.

If our clients had held that large piece of land in an LLC or a limited partnership though, things would have been different. Our clients could have distributed the second piece of property from one structure to a new structure at "basis." There would be no taxable event and nothing to base a capital gain on. The property simply moves out at whatever value it is held at on the books.

Charging Orders

Earlier we explained how using an LLC or a limited partnership can help to prevent a personal creditor from seizing assets that you hold in one of these entities. We told you that most states use the Uniform Limited Partnership Act or the Uniform Limited Liability Company Act, and that both of those acts offer some protection from creditors. But before you run out and put everything you own into an LLC, thinking you can now engage in some very risky ventures, we need to explain a little more about what rights creditors do have.

First of all, not every state uses the original versions of the Uniform Limited Partnership Act and the Uniform Limited Liability Company Act. Some states have modified these two Acts to provide more protection to a creditor, while others have not, or have strengthened the property owner's position. Some states allow creditors to make a special application to have LLC or limited partnership assets seized and sold. You will definitely need to take a look at your own state's laws to see what position your state takes, when you are planning your own asset protection strategy.

Second, just because these two Acts prevent many creditors from seizing and selling your LLC's or limited partnership's assets, that doesn't mean a creditor is completely out of luck. The idea of these two Acts and the asset protection they provide is that the government really doesn't want people to lose everything they own when they make a mistake. At the same time, however, a person who has been injured or wronged by that mistake, or who is owed money, also deserves some form of compensation. So the government came up with a compromise, called a Charging Order.

A *Charging Order* is part lien and part garnishing order. Where a lien is placed against property, a Charging Order is placed against your LLC or limited partnership interests. Where a garnishing order intercepts monies from your paycheck and diverts those monies to a spouse for alimony or child support, for example, a Charging Order can divert profits and distributions owed to you by an LLC or a limited partnership. A

Charging Order will stay in place for as long as you own the LLC or limited partnership interests, or until you have paid off the judgment in full, or it has been released by the judgment creditor. If you were to try to sell your LLC or limited partnership interests while a Charging Order was in force, you would either have to pay off the debt before the transfer could be completed, or the new owner would have to agree to take on the remaining debt owed to the Charging Order (which is pretty unlikely).

While on the face of it this sounds cumbersome and unappealing, there is one important thing to remember. In many states, placing a Charging Order against a property title is the ONLY remedy a creditor has. That creditor can only wait in line and hope that the LLC or limited partnership produces enough profit to pay off the judgment. It may take months, years, or even decades, and in many cases the idea of waiting for such a long time is a deterrent to creditors, meaning they would rather negotiate with you to settle a claim than go through the Charging Order process.

Right Answer 99 Percent of the Time

As we've repeated throughout this book, there is no one answer that is always right for all circumstances when it comes to legal and tax planning. However, there is one answer that is **almost** always right in determining the best entity to use to hold your property for tax purposes. For the reasons stated previously, we generally recommend that clients hold their properties in an LLC.

ACTION STEPS

1. What business structures do you currently use to hold your real estate investments?

2. Based on your review of the preceding information, are there any changes you need to make to your current business structures?

3. What action steps do you need to take immediately?

Chapter 5

TITLING PROPERTY: TENANCIES, TRUSTS, AND TRANSFERS

Now that we've talked about good business structures to hold real estate, let's talk about some of the tricky details, such as how you want to take, hold, and transfer title to real estate.

First, let's take a quick look at the ways you can hold title.

TITLING OPTIONS

■ **Joint tenancy.** This type of tenancy is often seen with married couples, because joint tenancy allows for each tenant to have undivided ownership and survivorship rights. Each tenant is considered to own 100 percent of the property. Undivided ownership is a double-edged sword, though. On the one hand it makes sure that one tenant cannot unilaterally sell his or her interest without first formally severing the tenancy and converting it to a tenancy-in-common. So in a marital breakdown, for example, it makes sure that one spouse can't sell the house out from underneath the other spouse. On the other hand it means that if either tenant is sued and has a judgment made against him or her, 100 percent of the property is at risk of being seized and sold by creditors.

- **Tenancy-in-common.** This is the most common form of shared ownership, and allows each tenant to own a separate portion of a property. An owner may sell or transfer his or her portion of ownership and the purchaser would simply assume the seller's role as a tenant-in-common. If an owner is sued or a creditor tries to attack that owner's assets, the creditor may go only after the portion of real estate that particular tenant owns, rather than 100 percent of the property.

Although we have been speaking in terms of couples, joint tenancies and tenancies in common can be between any number of individuals or entities. Here is a form of tenancy that is restricted to married couples:

- **Tenancy-by-entirety.** This type of ownership allows for couples to each hold a 100 percent interest in real property, but, unlike a joint tenancy, if one spouse's interest is attacked by a creditor, the other owner's interest remains unattached.

  This is a tenancy option that you must talk to your attorney about first. Not all states allow tenancies-by-entirety, and this type of tenancy does not always provide complete asset protection.

WROS—FOUR SMALL LETTERS THAT MAKE A BIG DIFFERENCE

The letters *WROS* mean "with right of survivorship," and it is absolutely crucial to make sure that you add these four letters to your title when you are selecting a tenancy option (i.e., Bob and Jane Doe, Joint Tenants, WROS).

The reason this is so important is that by using WROS, you are giving your approval to your interest in a property passing over to the other tenant without having to go through Probate. Probate is an expensive and time-consuming legal process to clear title on property or other personal goods before they may be transferred. Even if you have a will to make your wishes known, if you don't use WROS on your titles, that property will still be subject to probate.

TITLE AND BUSINESS STRUCTURES

In Chapter 4 we talked about business structures and how holding title to your real estate through a protected entity, such as an LLC or a limited partnership, could help to protect you and your assets in the event of a lawsuit. You can apply the same title and WROS principles we have just discussed to a business structure.

To do this, you need to apply the WROS to the ownership of the business structure, instead. So you may have a property held by the Smith Family LLC, with the Smith Family LLC owned by Jane and John Smith, JTWROS. Jane and John each own 100 percent of the LLC, which owns 100 percent of the property. Should either spouse pass on, the LLC will automatically become owned by the remaining spouse, without any probate or other outside interference.

Another good reason to make sure that couples set up their property title and LLC ownership this way is for tax purposes. We talked about this in Chapter 4, where we called the LLC set up this way a "disregarded entity" in the eyes of the IRS. This is a very good thing, because it allows you to keep things like the mortgage interest tax deduction, even though the property is now held by an LLC, and not you personally. So you get the tax benefits of home ownership, the tax benefits of a business, and the legal protection of an LLC—all in the same entity!

TITLE AND LIKE-KIND EXCHANGES

If you are a couple who are planning a possible like-kind exchange, it is better to title the property as tenants-in-common than to use the joint tenancy or single-member LLC option. Unrelated parties, friends, family, and so on should always use the tenants-in-common option. That is because the tenants-in-common method will allow one or more of the parties to sell their interest at a later date. Just imagine a situation where there are four partners and only three of them want to sell. If they used joint tenancy for their like-kind exchange they will be partners forever, or until they pay the legal and filing costs to sever the joint tenancy and convert that title to tenants-in-common.

However, there is still a way to hold the property and protect it in this situation. In this case you would want to make sure that the owners used their own individual LLCs instead of themselves personally. So instead of titling the property "John Doe and Jim Jones as Tenants-in-Common," you would have "John Doe, LLC and Jim Jones, LLC, as Tenants-in-Common." By titling the property in this fashion, you have protected the asset and complied with the new rules regarding multiple owners and like-kind exchanges.

A FEW WORDS ON TRUSTS

Trusts are very popular ways to hold assets and transfer wealth from one generation to the next. Used properly they provide great privacy, freedom from probate, and, for some states, a few extra benefits. Used improperly, they can leave your assets exposed to creditors.

The term *land trust* is used frequently in the real estate investor world. Did you know that there was more than one kind of land trust? That's an area that can cause confusion, especially if you aren't sure which type of land trust you are looking at or hearing someone talk about.

So, two quick definitions:

- A *land trust* has a Trustee, who controls all the business and profit distributions, and one or more beneficiaries, who are passive (like limited partners) and have no role in management. The trust holds the legal title to all assets for the beneficiaries, who hold the beneficial title, and the Trustee signs all documents, such as purchase and sale deeds, on behalf of the trust.
- An "Illinois-style" land trust also has a Trustee and beneficiaries, but their roles are reversed. The Trustee owns both legal and beneficial title to the property in the trust, and the beneficiaries act as day-to-day managers. The Trustee's role is usually limited to holding title and signing the occasional document, as the titleholder, while the beneficiaries do all

the work. This is very different; in fact, normally when a trust owns both legal and beneficial title to something, it isn't considered a trust by the law anymore and is dissolved. That's why Illinois-style land trusts aren't available in every state. Illinois-style land trusts do have one huge advantage over other trusts though, and that is the ease with which ownership can be transferred. A single signature is sufficient to transfer an Illinois-style land trust, and there are no formal recording requirements.

Trusts provide great privacy, because usually the only name associated with a trust is the Trustee. The underlying owners of the trust are usually not listed on any public records, even in an Illinois-style land trust, where the beneficiaries are doing all the work! This works well for high net-worth individuals, or celebrities, who don't necessarily want their portfolio to be an open book to the public. By making arrangements with an unrelated third-party individual or entity to act as the Trustee, these people make sure that their names aren't obviously associated with the Trustee, giving them some anonymity.

Trusts do not provide good asset protection, though. The problem is that trusts aren't considered legal entities by the Courts. They have no legal standing whatsoever. A court will just look right through a trust as though it didn't exist. That means if a trust that owns a property is sued, not only is all property held by the trust a potential asset for a creditor, but so are all the other assets of the trust's owner. That also means that if you are sued as an individual, the assets you hold in a trust are just as exposed as those you hold in your name directly.

However, if you use a combination of a trust and an LLC, you can have the best of both worlds. Instead of having the trust owned by its beneficiaries, have the trust owned by an LLC, that is in turn owned by the beneficiaries. Now if there is a lawsuit, either against the trust or against a beneficiary, the LLC asset protection rules come into play.

TITLE TRANSFER OPTIONS

There are three ways to transfer title: You can use a quitclaim deed, a grant deed, or a warranty deed.

- A *quitclaim deed* is the simplest and one of the most commonly-used documents. It simply records that you have quit your claim to title in favor of someone else.
- A *grant deed* transfers your ownership, but also implies certain promises; that is, that the property is yours to transfer, and that it is clear of liens and other charges, except for what you have set out in the document. A grant deed is also a very commonly-used document.
- A *warranty deed* also transfers your ownership and makes promises about the title, but unlike a grant deed, where promises are implied, in a warranty deed these promises are explicitly set out.

Although quitclaim deeds are one of the most common types of deeds used, and certainly the easiest to fill out, they aren't always a good choice. That's because quitclaim deeds completely sever title, and everything having to do with title, including the existing title insurance. This might not be a problem at the beginning, but imagine this: You buy a piece of property from a third party, obtain title insurance, and hold that property for a number of years, until you decide to do some asset protection and quitclaim the property to your new, single-member LLC. Your title agent is doing their due diligence before issuing new title insurance for the LLC, when they find a problem that had not been detected when you purchased the property from the third party. Perhaps the boundaries were incorrectly surveyed, or a hidden environmental hazard surfaces. The title company won't issue an insurance policy, and, because you quitclaimed the property to yourself, you cancelled your previous title insurance policy. You have no recourse against the original insurers and will have to bear the costs of fixing up the property yourself.

This problem can be avoided by using either a grant or a warranty deed, because in both cases the title insurance isn't extinguished by the deed, and even if it were, because you (or the owner, if it's not you transferring property to your business structure) made a promise that the title was good, the end purchaser has a fallback if a title problem occurs. And honestly, they aren't that much more difficult to complete from a quitclaim deed.

LET YOUR EXPERTS HELP!

Although you don't always need an attorney or a title company to help you prepare and file a property deed, it is a very good idea to let them do it anyway. The reason is simple: They are professionals who do this type of transaction every day and are aware of all the nuances and unexpected problems that might occur. What would happen if you prepared a deed incorrectly, had the seller sign it, and didn't find out that it was wrong until you went to record the deed at the local County Recorder's Office? For starters you would need to go back to the seller with a corrected deed. But what if the seller had moved in the meantime and had left no forwarding address? At the very least you would have a long process ahead of you, as you attempted to get the matter rectified, and it would probably involve legal fees and a court application. On the other hand, if you used an attorney or title agency and they made a mistake, you would still have a mess, but at least you'd also have the right to have someone else pay to have it fixed!

HOW TO PUT PROPERTY INTO AN LLC

This is always a huge question at speaking engagements and for clients generally.

If you have the opportunity ahead of time, we always recommend that when you are negotiating the purchase of a property, you make sure that you put into the contract that the property will be held in the name of "[blank], or [his/her/its] nominee." The nominee can then be the LLC or limited partnership that you (quickly!) form for that purpose. When the final papers are signed, you simply make sure that your nominee LLC or limited partnership is listed as the new owner and go from there.

If you can't have your LLC or limited partnership ready in time (on average it takes about two weeks to form an entity in most states, although many states are much faster), then you will have to take title initially in your own name and then transfer it into your entity's name. This can be expensive; you may have to pay the transfer tax and/or recording fees twice, as some states don't care that you own the entity, and beneficial ownership of the property really isn't changing. They just see that a transfer has occurred and a fee is now payable.

It can also be problematic if your bank sees that a title transfer has occurred and decides that the transfer invokes their "due on sale" clause, meaning that your mortgage financing will have to be redone also. While that doesn't sound like a serious problem (and many times it isn't), it can be if the bank doesn't want to lend money to your new business structure, because it has no assets or credit history. In this event, be prepared to sign a personal guarantee of the mortgage, even if it isn't in your name personally. This requirement will probably lessen as you invest in more properties and your business structure grows in value, but you can expect it in your early days.

And what if your mortgage lender doesn't want to lend to your business structure, even with a personal guarantee from you? Well, in that case, we suggest that you seek out another lender. There are many mortgage lenders who are happy to lend money to people who are engaging in proper asset-planning protection. In fact, from a bank's perspective it would seem a better bet to lend to someone who understands the risks and is taking steps to protect themselves! These lenders will just want to make sure that their own interests are taken care of, and as we said, that will probably require you to sign a personal guarantee.

ACTION STEPS

1. Review the records for the property you currently own. How are the properties held?

2. What, if any, changes do you want to make to the way you hold title on these properties?

3. Based on your review of this chapter, how do you want to hold property in the future?

4. What action steps do you want to take immediately?

Chapter 6

CLEVER USE OF DEBT

WHY DEBT?

I t is possible to buy real estate without debt. In fact, there are whole programs designed to find ways to pay off properties quickly. Some people feel that debt adds risk to owning property, but we actually feel that debt is the safest way to build wealth and to build it more quickly.

We use this example in another book, *An Insider's Guide to Making Money in Real Estate*, but it bears repeating. Let's assume that you have $100,000 that you can use to buy real estate. You invest in an area that appreciates at a very modest five percent per year. You have two choices: Plan A—buy a property for $100,000 cash or Plan B—buy a property for $1,000,000 with $100,000 as a down payment.

Now, fast-forward one year. The property has appreciated just as you have anticipated—at five percent. As a comparison, the Office of Federal Housing Enterprise Oversight, the federal body that tracks housing data, reports that the national average from the second quarter of 2003 to the second quarter of 2004 was 9.36 percent, the largest jump since the late 1970s, and that there are no signs that real estate appreciation will decrease or level off in the near future.

Leverage of Money—Risk or Reward?

A few years ago, a client of Diane's CPA firm wondered whether he should refinance his home to pull some money out. There was an investment property that he wanted to purchase, and he had calculated that a refinance could provide the funds for buying the property.

The real issue was that he and his wife were worried about the increased payment that would result from the refinanced amount. They would now have an extra $400 in payments each month. The new investment would allow them to buy a property that would give them a return of $1,000 per month. Of course, they would now have to make a payment of $400 each month to create that cash flow.

After going through all of their financial information, we determined that they needed six months' worth of expenses in their security bucket. A six-month cushion was established. They made the investment and everyone was happy!

Ironically, they sold their home for a big profit six months later and moved into another home. The investment appreciated much more than they had anticipated, so they soon had another $70,000 in equity on the property plus the cash flow as they had projected.

The amount held in their security bucket allowed them to move forward with confidence on their plan for wealth, and leverage of money created both cash flow and wealth.

Plan A means that your property has gone up in value to $105,000. You made $5,000. Not bad, but it did take $100,000 to do it. So you have a return on your money of five percent. Plan B, however, has now appreciated to $1,050,000. You made more than $50,000.

More debt does require more planning. What is your contingency plan? We strongly recommend that you prepare for debt by making sure you have adequate funds to ensure security for your family and to provide for emergency funds. At www.Dolfand Diane.com we further explain the concept of five baskets of income for financial planning for real estate investors:

1. Security.
2. Emergency.
3. Income.
4. Growth.
5. High-Risk.

Please check out our web site for this free e-book. As you continue to use debt, increase the amount of money you have in your security and emergency baskets so that you can build assets without fear!

DEBT IS ASSET PROTECTION

Apart from the extra leverage and financial gain advantages, debt protects the owner, while equity protects the lender. For example, if you have a property worth $1,000,000 and you owe $800,000, you have only $200,000 in equity at risk from frivolous lawsuits, bad tenants, and even foreclosure. However, if you

---

Why Debt?

Debt provides two big benefits for real estate investors:

1. Ability to leverage your money to grow wealth even faster.
2. Asset protection.

---

have that same property worth $1,000,000 and you owe nothing, you now have $1,000,000 at risk. High levels of debt give you more leverage and asset protection.

In fact, perhaps the worst thing you can do is to make extra principal payments on your loan. The extra payments don't help you if you miss a payment; the bank just gets more equity if they foreclose. Additionally, you've relinquished the financial boon of leverage.

Our recommendation is to frequently check in on the equity that your property is building. You typically build equity in one of three ways: (1) equity buildup through regular principal reduction on an amortizing note, (2) active appreciation—things you do to improve your property's value, and (3) passive appreciation— overall appreciation that occurs in a neighborhood.

APPLYING FOR MORTGAGES

Lenders look for the "three Cs" when they make loans:

1. Collateral.
2. Creditworthiness.
3. Cash flow.

Residential loans, which cover properties that have four or less units, are a little more flexible on terms for the borrower, because there are so many federally backed programs available. However, as you move into commercial loans (a term used to describe loans for multifamily properties of five or more units), the loan terms become more rigid. Lenders get very specific when they look at the three Cs. They will look at your creditworthiness, the collateral of the property, and the cash flow as evidenced by past performance. The less certain any of those three areas is, the more expensive the loan will be. That's why we commonly see a lower loan-to-value rate allowed for commercial properties. The lenders don't have the government backing that residential loans do, and so they want to see more equity in the property, and more collateral.

The three Cs method also explains why lenders are so reluctant to lend on vacant properties. There is no past performance to establish what the cash flow will be, so lenders only have the collateral and the creditworthiness of the borrower to review.

You can expect to pay a lot more in interest for these types of loans as well. As risk goes up, reward needs to go up as well. Lenders loan money according to that rule; make sure you follow it as you develop your investment strategies as well!

HOME MORTGAGES

The first debt for many real estate investors is their own home. As we have shown you, it is possible to use your home equity as a source for capital for investment in your next property.

There are some general rules about deductibility of home mortgage interest, however. As you proceed along the following rules, remember that if you use a home mortgage to buy a property, the interest on that mortgage loan would then be a deduction for the property being purchased. That means if you use a home equity line of credit to borrow $200,000 from your family home and then use that money to buy a rental property, the interest on the $200,000 from the loan is now a deduction against the rental property. If you use that $200,000 to buy a piece of property that you will be developing, because of the real estate developer issue, that interest would then need to be capitalized, just like any other cost for your development property. And, finally, if you use that $200,000 to buy a really cool boat, your interest would be deductible only to the extent that home equity interest can be deducted as set out next.

RULE FOR HOME MORTGAGE INTEREST DEDUCTIONS

Deductible mortgage interest includes the total acquisition indebtedness (not to exceed $1 million) and aggregate amount of home equity indebtedness not exceeding $100,000. This provision applies cumulatively to the total of both the principal residence and the second residence. Now, let's analyze what each of these terms actually means.

Acquisition Indebtedness

Under the definitions of the Tax Code, *acquisition indebtedness* is debt that is incurred in acquiring, constructing, or substantially improving the principal residence or a second residence of the taxpayer and is secured by such property.

This could become a problem for a homeowner who plans to

continue to refinance a home to provide funds for personal use. For example, assume that Carlos buys a principal residence in 2005 for $250,000, by putting 20 percent ($50,000) down and financing the rest. He now has a mortgage of $200,000. All the interest on this will be deductible, assuming that he itemizes on his personal return and high income doesn't start phasing out itemized deductions. The current level of phase-out for deductions is $139,500. Now, let's say that Carlos pays off the home over the next 10 years by paying extra on the loan. Then, he discovers he needs some money for personal expenses. So, he refinances his home to pull out the amount. He basically replaces the initial loan with a new loan of $200,000. The only problem is that the interest on the second loan is not tax deductible! The new loan was not considered acquisition indebtedness because the money wasn't used to buy the property. However, $100,000 would qualify as a qualifying home equity loan.

HOME EQUITY INDEBTEDNESS

Home equity indebtedness is debt that is secured by the taxpayer's principal or second residence and does not exceed the fair market value of such qualified residence after it has been reduced by the amount of acquisition indebtedness. In other words, the home equity indebtedness is the amount of debt on a property, after the acquisition indebtedness, as long as the total of the two types of debt does not exceed the fair market value. There is a cap on the deductibility of home equity indebtedness of $100,000. If you have a home equity loan that is more than $100,000, only the interest attributable to the first $100,000 will be deductible.

WHAT IS A PRINCIPAL RESIDENCE?

A principal residence includes a house, condominium, mobile home, motor home, boat, or house trailer that contains sleeping space, toilet, and cooking facilities. You can have only one qualified principal residence. You can also have one qualified second residence.

Home Mortgage Interest Deductions

As we keep saying, nothing is easy when it comes to the Tax Code. Here are the rules to fully deduct home mortgage interest deductions. You must:

- Make less than $139,500 (or your itemized deductions including the mortgage interest deduction will begin to phase out).
- Have debt of less than $1 million for acquisition of your home.
- Not have more than $100,000 in home equity debt.
- Be able to prove you used the acquisition debt to directly acquire or substantially improve your property.
- Have the debt secured by the property.

Note: None of these rules apply to debt for your rental properties.

WHAT IS A SECOND RESIDENCE?

A second residence, just like a principal residence, could be a house, condo, mobile home, motor home, boat, or house trailer, as long as it contains a sleeping space, toilet, and cooking facilities.

The definition of second residence starts to get a little fuzzy, however, when you rent it out. The mortgage interest and property tax will be only deductible on a second residence as long as the property meets the interest deductibility requirements.

The property is considered a second residence as long as you either (1) don't rent it out to anyone during the year or (2) personally use it at least two weeks a year, or 10 percent of the number of days the residence is rented out to others, whichever period is greater. The "rented out to others" period includes the time that the property is held out for rental or resale or is being repaired or renovated with the intention of then holding it out for rental or resale.

HOME RESIDENCE CHOICES

There are a couple of decisions to be made when it comes to your home residence if you have more than one property. Which property will be your principal residence and which will be your vacation home? If you have a vacation home, are you better off taking the deduction of interest and personal as a second residence, which assures the deduction, or meeting the rental requirements so that you get full value of the rental? You can find more about these questions (and our answers) in Chapters 10 and 11.

For now, though, consider how much you use leverage in your current plan. Maximize your interest deductions whenever possible. Sometimes the interest is not deductible. If so, what changes will make it deductible?

ACTION STEPS

1. List each property you own and the current total debt, plus interest rate.

2. Are you fully utilizing the debt in your property or are there additional leverage possibilities?

3. If you plan to utilize equity in your home in a loan, do you intend to have the mortgage interest deductible? If so, make sure that you keep a good paper trail on the source of funds.

4. We recommend that you set up a time for a regular review of your current leverage on all properties. For example, the authors regularly review all properties on at least an annual basis. What plan do you want to establish to review the leverage opportunities for your properties?

5. Based on your review of this information, what action steps do you want to take immediately?

Chapter 7

SELL YOUR PROPERTY WITHOUT IMMEDIATELY PAYING TAX

SHOULD YOU SELL?

Sometimes selling is the best alternative. But generally, we like to hold on to property. If you are buying and selling properties, you can take advantage of the gain, but then you have to start all over again building your wealth. On the other hand, if you keep properties that have appreciated and use leverage to access the equity instead of selling, you will get your money and will still have the asset. Remember there are three wealth-building results when you invest in real estate:

1. Creating cash flow.
2. Creating wealth through passive and active appreciation.
3. Creating tax advantages.

Sometimes selling is the best option if the investment is less than sound. If your main goal in selling is to get cash out of the deal, consider simply refinancing to access the cash.

How Much Is the Gain?

As we review the methods for deferring the gain from your property, remember that the amount of gain will be an important component. *Gain* is the sales price, minus the cost of sales, minus the basis. The basis is also impacted by the amount of accumulated depreciation on the property. There isn't a quick way to determine the amount of gain on property because the basis is not always a straightforward calculation.

Gain rarely equals the amount of cash you get when you sell a property. If you previously sold a property and deferred the gain into this property through a like-kind exchange, refinanced, made improvements, or owned the property for a long period of time, your cash from the sale will be substantially different.

SELL NOW, PAY LATER

There are three main ways that you can sell a property and pay tax at a later time. These are:

1. Installment sales method.
2. Like-kind exchange.
3. Pension plan purchase/sale.

Each of these three plans produces dramatically different results.

Installment Sale

An installment sale occurs when you sell a property and carry back the note yourself. The installment sales method allows you to pay tax as you receive payments. Simply put, if you have a basis in the property of $150,000 and sell it for $200,000, you will receive a gross profit of $50,000 in total. For every dollar of the $200,000 you receive, 25 percent of it will be profit ($50,000 divided by $200,000). As you receive payments, part will be for interest and part will be for principal. The interest portion is taxable as regular interest income. The principal portion will be 25 percent taxable as capital gains (either long-term or short-term). There are a few tricks to all of this that we cover next.

An *installment sale* is a sale where you will receive money over time. This could be in a number of forms:

- You could sell your property that is currently free and clear and carry back a note with a down payment.
- You could sell your property with the buyer assuming your existing mortgage or taking it "subject to" the existing financing. You could also "take back a second" by allowing the buyer to pay you over time for the equity they are buying. The term *take back a second* means that you will record a note as second behind the existing financing to secure the loan that your buyer will make to you.
- You could sell your property with the buyer taking out a new loan and with you taking back the second mortgage. You will be paid over time as payments are made on the mortgage.
- You could sell the property on a lease option program that is designed to actually be a sale.
- You could wrap the existing financing with a *wrap sale* or land contract that states that payments are made to you and then you (or your designee) are responsible for making the payments on the existing financing that you have.

While each of these methods appears very different, there is still one consistent fact. You have created an installment sale. You don't get all the money right away; you receive it in payments over a period of time.

Installment Treatment versus the Dealer Status Issue

The IRS allows, in certain circumstances, the installment treatment of gains. This means that you pay tax on the gain as you receive the money. The IRS doesn't guarantee that your gains will be treated in this manner. It merely ALLOWS this treatment in certain circumstances. This bears repeating; don't assume that you will receive the installment gains tax treatment if you sell via an installment plan. If the IRS finds that you are a real estate dealer, you might just have to pay all the tax right now even if you didn't receive the money. If you're a dealer, you will also have to pay self-employment tax (unless the purchase and sale are done within a structure that doesn't have self-employment tax such as an S corporation or C corporation) and you are not allowed to take the tax installment sales method.

Installment Sales Method Benefit

There really isn't a big tax or financial benefit to taking advantage of the installment sales method. You pay tax as you receive money. It seems like it's only fair. There is a major problem, however, if you have to pay tax before you receive money (i.e., if you are considered a real estate dealer). Beware of that problem!

Like-Kind Exchange

A *like-kind exchange* occurs when you sell a property and then buy another one. You can defer the gain on the tax by rolling it into the next property. There's a bit of work involved, which we explain next.

The IRS allows you to "sell now, tax later" when it comes to the sale of real estate investment property. These types of deferrals are known as like-kind exchanges, Section 1031 exchanges, or a Starker exchange. There are a number of specific rules regarding this method of deferring taxes from the sale of property. The key (and first) test that you must meet is the three general requirements for gain deferral under Code Section 1031:

1. There must be an exchange; something is sold and something is acquired in a specific manner.
2. The properties exchanged must be of a like kind.
3. The property transferred and the property received must be held for productive use in a trade or business or for investment.

Definition of Like-Kind

There seems to be a lot of misinformation regarding the definition of like-kind. The IRS tells us that the determination is made as to the nature and character of the property. It doesn't matter if the real estate exchanged on either side is improved or unimproved. A condo can be exchanged for an apartment building. A bare lot can be exchanged for a commercial building. The key is that both the property you are disposing of and the property you are acquiring must be investment properties.

Until recently, there was a big question mark about whether you could exchange an investment property for a principal residence. Congress finally addressed this problem in the 2004 Job Creations Act. The rule now is that you can exchange an investment property for your home. The tax loophole occurs when you take advantage of the tax-free gain exclusion that comes from selling your home that you have lived in for two of the previous five years. If you are married, you can sell your home and exclude $500,000 of gain. If you're single, you can exclude $250,000 of gain.

Here's how the new loophole works. Let's say that you have an investment property that will have a gain of $500,000 when you sell. The investment no longer makes sense and you want to sell it. You could roll it into another investment property, and thus delay paying gain. Or, under the new loophole, you could roll it into a new house that you move into. You have to keep the house for five years as your principal residence before you sell, and then you can take the gain exclusion. In our example, we assumed that you were rolling over $500,000. Since we know that most property goes up in value, we'll assume that this one does as well. You happily discover that you now have a gain of $800,000 when you sell your house. You'll pay long-term capital gains tax on $300,000 of the gain and you'll get $500,000 of it tax-free. That's assuming that you are married and filing a joint return. Otherwise, the gain is limited to $250,000.

Exchange Rules

The best advice anyone can give you is to make sure you have an Exchange Specialist or an Accommodator as part of your team during the exchange process. Generally, you will have a sale in process when you discover the possible properties you want to acquire. You are required to prepare a list of three properties within 45 days and close on the new property within 180 days of the sale of the first property.

You cannot take possession of the proceeds from the initial sale without incurring tax on that income. The money must be held separate from your other funds and used solely for the purchase of the new property.

The job of the Accommodator is to make sure that you comply with all the requirements of the like-kind exchange, plus to facilitate the transfer by serving as the go-between during the escrow process.

Basis for the Like-Kind Exchange

A simple like-kind exchange would be one in which one property is sold and one property is bought. All the proceeds of the property and the basis are "rolled" into the next property. If you have bought a new property for a higher sales price than you had sold the initial property for, you have a straightforward like-kind exchange. But when it comes to accounting for like-kind exchanges, nothing is straightforward.

First, you "roll" the basis of the initial property into the new one. Let's assume that you have a basis of $200,000 with accumulated depreciation of $50,000 in the building you sell for $500,000. You then buy a property for $600,000. For this demonstration we ignore any other issues that you would usually have to deal with (seller financing, impound accounts, deposits, and costs of both the sale and the purchase, to name a few) and concentrate only on the basis and its depreciation.

Your new basis in the property will be recorded as $300,000

with accumulated depreciation of $50,000. The $300,000 is calculated as:

$200,000 roll-over basis (which equated to $500,000 of the new property).

$100,000 additional basis you picked up as the difference between the sales price of $500,000 and purchase price of $600,000.

The depreciation will then continue, under whatever old system of depreciable lives had been used, for the $200,000. An accumulated depreciation balance of $50,000 is transferred. For this portion of the depreciation schedule, it's as if you never sold the initial property.

You will begin a new depreciation schedule for the $100,000 additional basis. This portion of the basis will follow the current depreciation lives and percentages.

Remember that you will need to back out the land value from the depreciable basis as well. We prorate the land value between the two portions of value. For example, if 20 percent of the value is determined to be in the land, then 20 percent of the total would be land. In this way, each portion of value is impacted.

Receiving Boot

It's possible to have a partial like-kind exchange where only part of the gain is tax deferred. This might be when you receive *boot*, which is generally cash or another consideration that is something different from the real property received.

An example would be where investment property with a basis of $50,000 is exchanged for real estate with a fair market value of $60,000 and cash in the amount of $20,000. The normal gain for this transaction would be calculated as $30,000 ($60,000 property + $20,000 cash – the basis of $50,000).

The gain, though, is recognized (and taxable) only to the amount of the cash actually received, or $20,000. The $20,000 is considered boot. The rest ($10,000) reduces the basis in the new property.

A reduction in liability can also be considered boot. This could happen when you sell a property and the loan is assumed. Beware! If you are contemplating a like-kind exchange, make sure you have all the details worked out ahead of time.

Multiple Properties in a Like-Kind Exchange

We have discussed only straightforward like-kind exchanges and already the accounting has gotten difficult!

There is one more potential accounting wrinkle. You can exchange one or more properties for one or more other properties. In the accounting world, we refer to that as A to B & C or A & B to C. Of course, it could be A & B to C & D, as well!

Does a Like-Kind Exchange Always Make Sense?

No, a like-kind exchange does not always make sense. Here are some examples of times you would not want to consider a like-kind exchange:

- **Property could be sold for a loss.** Take the loss against other income and then buy another property separately, if that is your plan.
- **Gain could be offset with other losses.** Exchanges generally cost more money than a regular sale. If you have current gain that could be offset by other losses, do a regular sale and offset the losses.

- **Liquidity is required.** Quick! You need cash. You can get cash out of a like-kind exchange, but the process is slow. You'll need to exchange into the new property, let the dust settle, and then refinance the new property. If you need money fast, that's not the best option.
- **You don't want another property.** The like-kind exchange assumes that you want a property. If you don't, then a like-kind exchange is not for you.
- **Tax hit is worth the additional basis.** The capital gains tax rate is always lower than your ordinary income tax rate. Don't assume that a like-kind exchange is always the best thing for you. It could be that it's worth it to pay tax now because your current tax rate is low and to avoid rolling over a reduced basis into another property. Done this way, the new property would have the regular basis, which could serve you well in the future.

Pension Plan Purchase/Sale

It's also possible to buy property in a pension plan, provided it's the right kind of pension plan. If your pension plan is one that works with real estate, you'll be able to defer the income and gains from real estate (if you have a regular pension plan) or get all the income and gains tax-free (if you have a ROTH plan). We have more on both of these plans next.

Using Pension Funds to Invest

First, here's the disclaimer. Not every kind of pension fund will allow real estate investing. For example, most 401(k) plans do not, although some of the new Sole 401(k) plans do. If you have a pension plan and are thinking of investing in real estate, check to see if your current plan allows real estate investing. If it does not, consider rolling the pension funds into a self-directed individual retirement account (IRA) that does allow for real estate investments. Remember also that the company that administers the self-directed plan will likely have a protocol that you will need to follow to invest in real estate. Make sure that you follow their procedures, to keep yourself safe.

Assuming that your pension plan allows for real estate investments, the easy way is to have your pension purchase real estate from an unrelated party and pay cash for the purchase. As long as you do not use the real estate for personal use while it is in the pension, there are no special issues.

A more difficult method for investing is to have your pension invest through a down payment and then leverage the rest. Here are the challenges:

- You cannot personally guarantee a loan for your pension.
- It may be difficult to get a bank to allow your pension to be the debtor without a personal guarantee.
- Your pension will pay tax on unrelated debt financial income (UDFI), which is the income and/or capital gains attributable to the leveraged portion.

If you can get through those challenges, however, here are some possible scenarios for investing with your pension:

- A self-directed IRA can be a member in an LLC or a limited partner in a limited partnership. There are some additional rules based on the percentage owned by pension plans.
- A self-directed plan is buying a property with a note. The plan will be subject to UDFI tax on any income attributable to the leveraged portion on the investment.

- A self-directed plan buys an option for a property. A pension fund can buy an option on a property from an unrelated party. In this case, a sibling will be exempted. The box on the opposite page is an example of how an option in a pension plan could work.

What a Pension Plan Cannot Do

Here are a few more restrictions to bear in mind when thinking about using pension funds to invest:

- You may not personally own property that you intend to purchase with pension plan funds.
- You must ensure that your intended purchase is not a prohibited transaction.
- The property must be purchased for investment purposes only.
- Neither you, your spouse, nor family members (except for siblings) may have owned the property prior to its purchase.
- Neither you nor your family members (other than siblings) may live in or lease the property while it's in the pension plan.
- Your business may not lease or be located in or on any part of the property while it's in the pension plan.

How Is the Pension Fund Taxed?

Real estate earnings will be taxed according to your specific type of pension plan. If you have a self-directed IRA that owns the real estate, then the property will have tax due upon distribution. If, on the other hand, you have a self-directed ROTH plan, the income and gain will be tax-free.

Tom has found a great deal! It's a real fixer upper and he could do the work, but he has a problem. He can afford the down payment and will qualify for the loan, but he doesn't have the money to do the fix-up and to hold the property while it's under construction. The house will cost $100,000, and will easily be worth $200,000, once the work is done. Tom estimates the materials will cost about $20,000.

His friend John has a suggestion. John has some money in his pension fund that has been steadily losing value. He's ready to invest it in a better deal, and this sounds like it!

Tom agrees to buy the home and do the work. He would like to get $20,000 for his work and then split the profit of $60,000 ($200,000 − 100,000 − 20,000 − 20,000 = $60,000). John agrees with the terms and directs his IRA to buy an option for $20,000 to buy the home for $150,000.

When the property sells (assuming the $200,000 sales price), several things happen: John's IRA does a simultaneous close to buy the house for $150,000 and sell it for $200,000. John's IRA paid $20,000 for the option up front, so it will receive a gain of $30,000. His $20,000 turned into $50,000 and he's ready for the next deal! Tom receives $150,000 from John's IRA. His gain is $50,000, representing $20,000 for his work and $30,000 for his share of the profit. The $20,000 he received for the option was used to complete the repairs and sell the property. Not bad for a four-month effort!

Sell Now, Pay Later

There are four ways to sell and pay tax later:

1. **Installment sales method.** This is not really a tax-savings device. It's just a way to match up cash with tax. BEWARE! If you're a real estate dealer, you cannot take advantage of this tax method.
2. **Like-kind exchange.** You'll defer the tax until you sell the next property with this method. But you'll also reduce your basis and depreciation over time. Don't always default to a like-kind exchange.
3. **Pension plan.** If you buy property in a pension plan and then sell it, the proceeds will be held within the pension plan. If you have a regular deferral-type pension plan, you'll pay tax when you take the money out of the plan.
4. **ROTH pension plan.** You can also buy property in a ROTH pension plan. The ROTH allows you to make money and not pay tax. A ROTH is a "tax never" plan.

ACTION STEPS

1. What is your current plan for taking money out of your investment properties?

2. How much tax do you anticipate paying on the income or gain that results from profit?

3. What strategies could you put in place to delay or reduce your taxes?

4. Based on the information contained in this chapter, which methods for deferring or avoiding tax would work for you?

5. What action steps are you prepared to commit to that will increase the money you make and reduce your taxes?

Chapter 8

AVOIDING THE TICKING TAX BOMB

ALTERNATIVE MINIMUM TAX—
PROBLEM NOW, DISASTER LATER

The Alternative Minimum Tax (AMT) was designed as an alternative tax for the very wealthy, who were able to take advantage of tax loopholes. At the time it was originally put into law, these individuals were able to use tax loopholes to completely offset all income and pay no tax. That's why this tax was designed. It was a way to make sure that all Americans paid something!

Fast-forward to today: The tax loopholes have kept coming. In fact, the best tax loopholes come when you invest in real estate. You no longer need to be rich to take advantage of these loopholes. That means more people are also becoming susceptible to the AMT.

Inflation continues to push income upward. This increase in taxable income is called *bracket creep*. Income tax brackets have been adjusted to take inflation into account. AMT brackets, however, have not. More middle-income people (as many

119

as 17 million people!) will soon become subject to the AMT. In fact, if you make more than $50,000 per year, plan on starting to worry about the AMT soon.

It's a ticking tax bomb for unsuspecting American taxpayers. The AMT is also an important part of any discussion regarding tax planning. That's because the normal tax planning techniques cannot protect you against the AMT. The rules are different.

What Is an AMT?

An AMT is an alternative type of tax. The AMT tax rate is applied against AMT taxable income. This is where the problem comes in. Items that are legal deductions for ordinary income tax are not deductions for AMT purposes.

There are two AMT tax rate brackets: 26 percent and 28 percent. The rates will be applied to the new AMT income base. The two amounts—the AMT tax and the income tax—are then compared. You will pay whichever is higher.

So the best income tax planning in the world for regular taxes won't help you if the AMT kicks in. At a minimum, you'll have to pay the AMT tax.

Filing Requirements

Form 6261—Alternative Minimum Tax for Individuals—is a complicated form that is used to report your AMT calculation. The IRS estimates that this form will take more than six hours to complete. And, the worst news of all, you might need to complete this form even if you don't need to pay the tax!

Calculating the AMT

The AMT is computed by starting with the regular taxable income from your individual tax return, Form 1040. You then increase or decrease the taxable income with the AMT adjustments and tax preference items.

Some examples of adjustments are:

- Taxes claimed as itemized deductions.
- Accelerated depreciation.
- Capital gains tax rates.

AMT Depreciation Issues

AMT depreciation is calculated using a different depreciation method, recovery period, and convention. It's necessary to keep track of AMT depreciation in a separate schedule from the schedule for regular depreciation. The AMT depreciation slows down the rate at which the property is depreciated. This method will produce smaller depreciation deductions and larger AMT adjustments in the earlier years in which property is in service, and larger deductions and smaller adjustments in later years.

If you have had to use the AMT depreciation for your property, its adjusted basis must be computed under AMT rules to determine the gain or loss from the sale, and the difference between the regular tax gain or loss and the recomputed AMT gain or loss becomes an adjustment in the year of sale.

One way you can avoid the AMT depreciation adjustment is to elect to use straight-line depreciation or 150 percent declining balance depreciation for all property for both regular tax and

AMT purposes. These depreciation methods will ultimately create the same total amount of depreciation. The straight-line depreciation and the 150 percent declining balance depreciation will have lower depreciation allowances in the beginning of the term but will increase over time. There might be some benefits to following this system because it will simplify your accounting and also guarantee that you will not become subject to the AMT as a result of a later sale of the property. There will be a tax cost of making this election, however, because the depreciation will be reduced initially.

Another strategy is to take advantage of the netting rules that apply in computing the AMT adjustment to avoid becoming subject to the AMT. Depreciation for all property is combined in calculating AMT income, allowing the netting of excess regular tax deductions for property that is recently placed in service with excess AMT deductions on property placed in service in earlier years.

Here's an example of how that would work. Assume that you have two buildings. One is old and one is new. In determining the regular tax liability, the new building will get you $5,000 in depreciation and $4,000 under AMT depreciation. The old building will get $7,500 in depreciation under regular depreciation rules and $9,000 under the AMT depreciation system. The total for the regular depreciation would be $12,500 ($5,000 + $7,500) while the AMT depreciation would be $13,000 ($4,000 + $9,000).

One final strategy involves planning for an AMT hit. If an asset has a separate AMT basis, you could sell the asset in an otherwise AMT year and reduce the tax on the gain. Here's how it could work. Let's assume that you have an asset with a regular basis of $100,000 and a basis of $150,000 for AMT purposes.

(Remember the AMT depreciation is less in the beginning, so your basis will be higher.) Now let's assume that you sell the property for $200,000. This would create a capital gain of $100,000 in a regular tax year. If you had a 31 percent tax rate (we're blending the ordinary tax rate for the recaptured depreciation with the capital gains rate), you would have a total tax due of $31,000. Now instead assume that you sold the building in your AMT year with its AMT basis of $150,000. The tax due under the AMT would be $13,000 ($50,000 gain × 26 percent AMT tax).

Passive Activity Losses under AMT

Passive activity losses, which include real estate losses, are first adjusted to eliminate any tax preference items, such as accelerated depreciation. The loss limits are then allowed only to the income limitation. There is no exception for real estate professionals in this case.

One strategy to avoid a problem is to purposely create a business or real estate dealer situation if you expect a loss. The business loss would not be considered a passive activity loss, and so there would be no limitations.

If you have passive activity losses, avoid AMT years. In years where the AMT is inevitable, avoid passive activity losses.

AMT adds a new wrinkle to tax planning. The best defense is a good understanding and proactive strategies to first identify when AMT is an issue and then develop the most comprehensive plan to limit the risk from the tax.

Of course, we can also hope that Congress changes the rules soon so that this ticking time bomb doesn't go off for you!

ACTION STEPS

1. Review your past year's tax return. Were you subject to the AMT last year?

2. What changes in income do you expect for this year? Will this make you subject to the AMT? (*Hint:* Do this as a check-in as early in the year as possible to make sure you have plenty of time to plan for the AMT, if that is a possibility.)

3. What systems do you have in place to ensure that the AMT doesn't sneak up on you?

4. What action steps do you want to take immediately?

Chapter 9

EXIT STRATEGIES

WHAT IS YOUR EXIT STRATEGY?

Know what you're doing before you buy a property. And, for that matter, know what you're doing before you sell a property or exchange one. If you can always start with the end in mind, you'll be better prepared to avoid unintended tax results.

POSSIBLE EXIT STRATEGIES

Following is a sample of some possible exit strategies for real estate properties. Your own plan might not be listed, but whatever your plan, make sure you've reviewed the financial and tax consequences. Plus, make sure you know what your Plan B is, in case your first plan doesn't work out.

Quick Sale

First of all, we want to say that we have nothing against quick sales of property. These sales, also known as flips, can be a great source of cash to buy property you want to hang on to. But remember that these deals will generally be considered trade or business income, so you will be considered a real estate dealer. That means the income you make will be ordinary income.

Rent to Own

We've mentioned the Rent to Own Program only briefly so far, although we discuss it in greater detail in later chapters. The benefits of this plan are that you get higher than normal returns. You will also need to make sure that the contract will have specific language so that it is clearly defined as a rental, and not a sale. That way, you'll be able to defer tax on the option payments that you will receive. Probably the biggest challenge that you may experience with this plan is finding tax advisors who understand the benefits of creative real estate investments.

Cash Cow

Your entire plan may be to create a stream of income from your property either now in the form of positive cash flow, or later, when the property appreciates and you can refinance to access the equity. This is called a *holding strategy*. There is still the question of what the exit strategy will be on the property. If nothing else, at some point you will need to determine who will inherit the property upon your death. Sometime, somehow, there is a point where you will no longer own this property. What is your exit strategy? Sometimes we get so focused on getting results right now, that we forget what the ultimate goal will be with a property. We cover some gift and estate tax options later on in this chapter.

Pay Off the Property

For some people, the ultimate security is to pay off their investment properties. The cash flow improves because there is no
longer any payment on the property. It is true that the very
wealthiest in the nation frequently use cash to purchase their
homes. By the way, note that we said "homes" because it's not
unusual for some to have an apartment in Paris, a penthouse in
Manhattan, and an estate in Phoenix. We probably left out a few
choice destinations, but the point is that the wealthy often own
more than one home and they generally pay cash for them. Face
it, if you have $4 billion that gives you even a small five percent
return . . . what would you do with all the money anyway? It just
becomes too much of a hassle to worry about getting a mortgage.

For everyone else, leverage becomes a way to build wealth. It
is true that you will increase your cash flow when you pay off
your property, but you will also slow down the velocity of your
money. Paying off your loan also means building up more equity
that is now a target for frivolous lawsuits.

That all aside, though, paying off the property is still not an
exit strategy for the property. At some point, you won't own it.
What do you want to do with it?

Gift

Perhaps your ultimate goal is to give the property to family members or to a charity. Start planning now to give gifts in the best
leveraged way. The current gift tax limitation for any donor is
$11,000 per recipient per year. That means that you can give
$11,000 of cash or property to someone in any one year, and
there will be no gift tax due. If you're married and have two children, as a couple you could give a total of $44,000 away per year

127

under this plan (calculated as $11,000 to each child from you, and $11,000 to each child from your spouse). If you give appreciated property, your basis in the property will be used to determine the gift amount.

For example, if you have a property with a basis of $40,000 and debt of $30,000 that is now worth $200,000, your gift value for gift tax purposes would be $10,000 ($40,000 – $30,000). But what if your property basis is more than $11,000? One strategy is to put the property into a family limited partnership (that's the same as a regular limited partnership, it's just owned by family instead of unrelated parties), and then annually gift a percentage of that partnership to your child. It is also possible to give more than $11,000 per year using this method. Be warned, though. The family limited partnership has recently come under fire from the IRS for the minority discounts. A minority discount reduces the value of the gift because the minority partnership interest is deemed to have less value than a similar interest percentage that has voting power. You are safe giving $11,000 in value under this method, but you may have a problem using discounted values to give larger annual gifts.

Another method is to sell the property to your intended gift recipient. Take back a note on the sale. Each year, you will forgive a portion of the note. For example, let's say that you sell a property for $200,000 for a note for the full value. To keep our example simple, we'll assume that there is no debt on the property. The IRS tells us we must use an interest rate or they will "impute" one for us. So we set an interest rate of five percent per year. In the first year, you can forgive $11,000 of the note ($10,000 for interest and $1,000 for principal). If your child is married and you have given the property to both, you will be able to forgive $22,000 ($10,000 for interest and $12,000 for principal).

What Is Your Exit Strategy?

Before you buy your property, know what your exit strategy will be. You could:

- Sell.
- Rent to own.
- Give it to an heir eventually.
- Give it to charity eventually.
- Give it now.

If you don't choose, circumstances may decide for you!

Another strategy that we recommend for anyone who has property they want to sell in a few years is to use the property to pay for a child's college tuition. If your child is over 14 years old, gift the property to them and let them sell it! The child would most likely pay tax at a lower rate on the sale. There is also a big tax loophole currently on the books that is scheduled to occur in 2008. If you are within the two lowest tax brackets in 2008, you will have a zero percent capital gains tax rate that year. Maybe that would be a great time for your child to sell the property to pay for college!

EXITING OUT OF A LIKE-KIND EXCHANGE

In a like-kind exchange, the exit strategy becomes even more important. That is because the property will have a reduced basis due to the rollover of deferred gain. The property has less depreciation and less life left to depreciate the asset. At some point, the tax advantages will be gone on a like-kind exchange. If you do another like-kind exchange, you just roll your tax problem over to another property. What is your exit strategy from a like-kind exchange?

There is a special type of trust called a Charitable Remainder Trust (CRT), that could help you, if you are facing this problem.

Charitable Remainder Trust

A CRT has long been used to avoid capital gains tax on highly appreciated assets. A CRT also allows you to accomplish personal and financial goals. As such, they are commonly used by the wealthy as a way to distribute wealth.

There are two main steps in creating a CRT. First, make sure you have a knowledgeable attorney establish a CRT that will qualify under the Internal Revenue Code as a charitable trust and exempt from taxation. Then, give your appreciated assets to the trust. This transfer will create an immediate income tax deduction that you can use on your personal tax return. The tax deduction will be based on a calculation of the future gift to a charity based on the interest payout you have selected, the government discount rate at the time of the transfer, and the term of the trust. If you can't use all the charitable deduction in the first year, you can roll it over to the next five years.

After the property has been transferred, you can sell the property and reinvest the proceeds. There would be no tax due on the sale because a charity is the ultimate recipient. The entire proceeds can then be invested to create a stream of income that you will receive. Upon your death, the charity becomes the beneficiary of the trust.

> ### Your Three Choices for Your Estate
>
> If you have a taxable estate when you die, there will be three possible beneficiaries:
>
> **1.** The heirs you want to have inherit it.
> **2.** Charitable institutions.
> **3.** The IRS.
>
> You get to pick two. If you don't pick, the IRS will choose for you. And guess which one it will choose!

EXITING OUT OF LIFE

As you build wealth, it's only natural that at some point you'll ask yourself what you really want to do with it. If you don't choose, the government chooses for you. Before you die, you have a choice of either giving the wealth away while you are alive, or giving it away when you die.

Estate planning is a huge subject for another book, but there are some basics to consider as you develop your personal exit strategy. What do you want to have happen with the wealth you accumulate? If you want to give it to your heirs, then you can easily accomplish that by waiting until you die, as long as you realize that they will get only what's left after the IRS takes their share. Alternatively, you can begin to gift your assets to them now, taking advantage of the annual gift tax exclusion.

Gift planning involving real estate can be accomplished by selling the property to an heir and then forgiving annual debt payments, creating a family limited partnership to gift discounted minority shares and maximizing the gift amounts or simply out-right gifts that may or may not have some gift tax.

If you'd rather have some of your estate go to charitable insti-tutions, consider some of the following methods:

- Charitable remainder trusts.
- Charitable lead trusts.
- Family foundations.
- Wealth replacement trusts.

Whatever you choose to do with the individual properties you buy and the wealth you accumulate, make sure you have a writ-ten plan that others know about. Perhaps the worst thing of all that can happen is that your plans, with the best of intentions, are never followed because no one else knew what you wanted.

ACTION STEPS

1. What is your current exit strategy for the properties you cur-rently own?

2. Do you have a backup plan in case that exit strategy does not work out?

3. Have you and your family reviewed each individual estate plan with others?

4. What action steps do you want to take immediately?

PART III

Home Loopholes

Chapter 10

BE PAID TO LIVE IN YOUR HOME

HOME SWEET HOME

We've already discussed the requirements to receive a mortgage interest deduction for your principal residence. If you have more than one home, the question becomes "How do you decide where your home really is?"

This had been an important issue for some states with high state income tax who are next to other states with lower, or even no state income tax. California and Nevada are good examples of this. To help stop the squabbling, the IRS stepped in and came up with a list of six factors that can help determine where your residency actually is:

1. Taxpayer's place of employment.
2. Principal place of abode of the taxpayer's family members.
3. Address listed on the taxpayer's federal and state tax returns, driver's license, automobile registration, and voter registration card.

4. Taxpayer's mailing address for bills and correspondence.
5. Location of the taxpayer's banks.
6. Location of religious organizations and recreational clubs with which the taxpayer is affiliated.

There is often no clear answer when you are reviewing the location of your principal residence. If challenged, you'll need to prove what your intent really was. If you plan to sell a highly appreciated property as a principal residence, make sure you've done all you can to meet the requirements.

LIVING IN YOUR ASSET

Are you paying for your house? Or do you have a plan so that it will pay you? Every homeowner who bought at a good price is sitting on tax-free money right now. Perhaps you are in a market that has gone down, but you know that you bought lower than most of your neighbors. If that's the case, then you know that when the market turns around, you'll be sitting well. Or maybe you are already safe in the knowledge that your house is your biggest asset because it has appreciated so well.

It isn't truly an asset unless it puts money into your pocket. But it could be the source of building a tremendous asset base for you. And you can do it tax-free!

The IRS lets you sell your principal residence in which you have lived for two out of the past five years and take out the gain tax-free up to $500,000 if you are married filing jointly or $250,000 if you are single.

Previous Law

We are still amazed at how many U.S. taxpayers aren't aware of the greatest tax gift Congress has ever given us. That tax gift is the ability to build up equity in your personal residence and then sell it without paying taxes. The previous law, which unfortunately, is still believed to be current, stated that you had to reinvest in a more expensive house unless you had reached a certain age.

The new law, enacted in 1997, says that if you live in your house for two of the previous five years, you can take advantage of the tax-free income. You don't have to buy another house. You don't have to be a certain age to take advantage of this change. It is available to every homeowner in the country.

Calculating the Two-Year Holding Period

When calculating the two-year holding period, let's first look at when the five-year period starts. The five-year period runs backward from the date of the sale of the property. During that five-year period you must have personally used the property for two years, or 730 days. Short temporary absences for vacations or seasonal absences are counted as periods of use, even if you rent out the property during these periods of absence. Keep those absences to under a year, though! Any absence more than one year is not considered a temporary absence.

For a married couple, the ownership test is met if either spouse meets the ownership test. However, if one of the spouses has taken advantage of this on another property within the previous two years and has taken a tax-free gain on a property sale, the couple must wait two years to take full advantage of this exemption on the current property. Otherwise, the gain exclusion is limited to $250,000 (the amount of exclusion for a single taxpayer).

What If I Don't Live in It for the Mandatory Two Years?

The IRS provides for hardship relief in certain cases where a taxpayer has to sell their home prior to the two-year time frame. The IRS tells us (at IRC Section 121) that

> ... if the sale or exchange of the residence is due to a change in the taxpayer's place of employment, health, or, to the extent provided in regulations, unforeseen circumstances, a taxpayer who does not otherwise qualify for the exclusion is entitled to a reduced exclusion amount.

Unforeseen circumstances include:

- Death.
- Disability.
- Becoming eligible for unemployment compensation.
- Change in job.
- Change in self-employment.
- Divorce.
- Multiple births from the same pregnancy.

Obviously, some of the unforeseen circumstances are easier to establish than others!

The *reduced exclusion amount* means that you can then exempt an amount equal to either the pro rata portion of time lived in the house times the total possible gain exclusion, but no more than the total gain. In other words, let's say that John and Corrine had lived in their home for only one year and had reason under this clause to qualify for the special circumstances. The fraction allowable would be 50 percent (because they had lived in the home for only 50 percent of the required time), so John and Corrine could take an exemption for $250,000 only (half of the possible $500,000 gain). If they had a gain of $100,000, they could exclude all of it. If they had a gain of $300,000, they only could exclude $250,000.

Unmarried Partners as Owners

If two partners are not married, but both share the same principal residence and are both on the title, then the tax-free exclusion will be $250,000 for each, provided they have met the two out of the past five year rule.

Home Exclusion after Divorce

When a spouse moves out of the residence and a divorce or legal separation process is started, it can sometimes take years to complete the process. The principal residence is either (1) sold immediately, (2) transferred in whole to one spouse, or (3) some hybrid plan that allows one spouse to live there for a period of time, but requiring a sale in the future that will benefit both spouses. If the home is sold immediately, the full gain exclusion would be allowed. If the transfer is made in whole to one spouse, then the exclusion for a single taxpayer would be allowed. However, in an interesting reversal of position, the IRS now says that if ownership is given to one spouse for a period of time (say until the children graduate from high school) and then sold, the noncustodial parent is now allowed the tax-free gain exclusion for the property as long as the whole arrangement was outlined in a divorce or settlement agreement.

CALCULATING GAIN ON SALE OF A PRINCIPAL RESIDENCE

Gain is calculated as:

Sales price – Selling expenses – Adjusted basis

Sales Price

The sales price is calculated by adding the total consideration received, liabilities assumed, and fair market value of other property received. Most of the time the sales price will be listed on the Uniform Settlement Statement, commonly known as a HUD-1.

Selling Expenses

The selling expenses associated with the sale of a personal residence include the expenses incurred to consummate the sales transaction, such as the real estate commission and title insurance. These expenses are listed on the HUD-1 as well.

Adjusted Basis

Basis plays an important part in calculating the gain of a property, yet it is often misunderstood. The basis begins with the price you paid for the property and then is adjusted by items such as:

Additions to basis:
Construction, reconstruction, and capital improvements.

Reductions to basis:

Insurance payments for casualty losses.

Deductible casualty losses not covered by insurance.

Previous partial sales of property.

Rolled-over deferred gain from pre-1997 home sales.

BUSINESS USE OF YOUR HOME

If you have a business or invest in real estate, chances are you have an office in part of your home. You have a legitimate deduction for a home if you can prove that you have:

- Exclusive business use of the space.
- Regularly conduct business in the space.

This deduction is a great way to write off expenses that you normally wouldn't be entitled to take, such as a portion of your homeowner's insurance, utilities, private mortgage insurance, homeowner's dues, and the like. The amount you can take depends on the percentage of your home's total square footage that is taken up by your home office. For example, if your home office takes up 10 percent of your home, then 10 percent of those costs are now a legitimate business deduction.

There is one other reason that you might consider having the home office as a deduction. Having your business in your home means that your "nondeductible commuter miles" are now just a short stroll down the hall. Everything from that office to other places of business is then completely deductible. You've just picked up a lot more business use of your home.

141

We used to have a concern that if you put a home office in your home, part of your gain would become taxable when you sell. For example, if 10 percent of your property was used as a home office, then 10 percent of the gain upon sale was now business related and thus taxable. No more! The IRS now says that if the home office is part of the residence, then you do not need to apportion gain to the home office.

The same rule is applicable if you rent out rooms in your house. For example, in high-cost San Francisco, a client of Diane's CPA firm has bought her first house. In order to afford the very high payments, she rents out rooms to friends. She's already seen more than $100,000 in appreciation in less than a year. When she sells, she'll be able to take her gain tax-free (up to $250,000 if she's still single, $500,000 if she marries by that time and her spouse qualifies). She's gotten into a high-priced market with the help of some renters and will be able to collect some tax-free money as a great reward!

You will be required to recapture the depreciation you took for the rented rooms or home office when you sell.

LOSS ON YOUR PRINCIPAL RESIDENCE

What if the unthinkable happens and your home goes down in value? The best advice is probably to wait it out and sell when the real estate market takes an upswing. There are many areas in our country, such as parts of California and Arizona, where the real estate market can have wild fluctuations. If you find yourself in a downswing, wait for the upswing!

There could be circumstances when you don't expect the market to turn back for your house or a situation where you just have to sell. In either case, and there is absolutely no other alternative, you may get stuck with a loss that you can't take on your tax return.

You are not allowed to take the loss on your principal residence, but you can take a loss on a business or investment property. So one strategy could be to convert your depreciated home into a rental property, making sure it legitimately can be characterized as such, and then sell it for the lesser value. The loss would be calculated as the sales price less the cost of the sale minus the basis. The basis would be what you had invested in the house during the time you owned it personally. In this way, you could take a deduction for the loss.

WHAT IF GAIN EXCEEDS TAX-FREE AMOUNT?

And here's the best problem of all! What if your gain exceeds the exclusion ($250,000 for single, $500,000 for married filing jointly) amount? Beside the obvious answer of "pay the tax and throw a really big party," you could also consider converting your home into a rental property. If the property legitimately is converted (with renters and proven history), then you could do a like-kind exchange to exchange the property into another property.

STRATEGY FOR HIGHLY APPRECIATED RENTAL PROPERTY

Finally, you can use this gain exclusion as a strategy for highly appreciated rental property that you want to sell. Normally, you would have to pay either capital gain or roll the gain into another property through a like-kind exchange. But with the gain exclusion strategy, you could move into the property for two years and then take the gain out tax-free up to the limits. Remember you will have to pay tax on the recaptured depreciation. Also note that if you are selling a multiunit complex, this strategy doesn't work, as only the part that is your principal residence will count.

RECORDKEEPING FOR PRINCIPAL RESIDENCES

Even though we have a great tax gift from Congress in the tax-free gain exclusion, it is still necessary to keep some records. Don't just assume that your gain will be less than the exclusion amount and so you won't need to prove anything to the IRS.

There is another tax benefit from home ownership that you receive each year, and yet, surprisingly, many people don't take advantage of it! The General Accounting Office released a frightening statistic in 2002. They had reviewed one million tax returns and compared them with the records that they had received independently. They found that more than one-half of those returns had been incorrectly prepared and estimated that Americans overpay their taxes by a half-billion dollars a year. The single biggest mistake that was made was the failure to properly itemize their principal residence expense of mortgage interest and property tax. People simply didn't take the deduction. Keep track of your records so you don't pay one more cent in taxes than your legal obligation.

We recommend that you keep a set of files for your principal residence called permanent files. The permanent files will have all the documentation related to the basis of the property, including:

- Closing statements from the purchase of the home.
- Rollover basis from a previous sale and purchase. If a previous home was sold pre-1997 and the basis was rolled into

the current home, you will need to know this rolled over amount for calculation upon a sale.

- Receipts and contracts related to additions and improvements.
- Any documentation related to partial sales of some of the property.

Additionally, keep copies of insurance policies, property tax information, and any other pertinent information for the property.

PERSONAL CONVERSION TO RENTAL

It's also possible that you might convert your personal residence into a rental at some later date. If you haven't calculated your basis in the property prior to conversion to rental, you will now need to do so. The basis will roll over to the new rental property.

ACTION STEPS

1. Are you comfortable that you have sufficient recordkeeping for your personal residence? If not, what changes do you need to make?

2. Do you know the basis for your home?

3. What is the exit strategy for your current home?

4. What action steps do you want to take immediately?

Chapter 11

VACATION PROPERTY

SECOND HOME OR RENTAL PROPERTY?

If you have a vacation home, is it a second home or a rental property? Which plan will give you the best tax loopholes?

If you have a second home, you might be able to deduct the mortgage interest and property tax as an itemized deduction. If the second home is not a rental, and total acquisition indebtedness for both the vacation home and principal residence is not more than $1 million and your total income as a married couple, filing jointly, does not exceed $139,500 (in 2004), you will have the deduction.

On the other hand, if the property is considered a rental, you'll be able to depreciate the property and deduct mortgage interest, property tax, utilities, homeowner's dues, repairs, and even travel to the property to inspect it. Of course, these deductions will be allowed only if the property is actually a rental under the IRS definitions. If the property ends up showing a loss, the loss would be treated like any other passive activity loss. In other words, you must have material participation, and your income levels must not stop you from being able to take the deduction. A real estate professional designation will make the income issue go away.

147

DEFINITION OF A SECOND HOME

First, let's review what it takes to be a second home. A property is considered a second residence as long as you either (1) don't rent it out to anyone during the year or (2) personally use it at least two weeks a year or 10 percent of the number of days the residence is rented out to others, whichever period is greater. A residence is considered to be rented during any period that the taxpayer holds the residence out for rental, resale, or repairs or renovates the residence with the intention of holding it out for rental or resale.

Here are some examples:

You own a second property and rent it out for 30 days. Your personal use is one week. It's a vacation home.

You own a property and rent it out for 30 days and also hold it out for rental for 200 more days. Your personal use is one week. It's a rental property.

Vacation Home Problem for Newlywed

If you and your spouse just got married, congratulations! If both of you owned a home and one (or both) of you owned a vacation home, you will be able to take deductions for only two homes. The solution for you here would be to convert one or more of your properties to rental properties, or sell.

CHALLENGES WITH TURNING IT INTO A RENTAL

Besides the issue of the number of days that a property is used personally versus the total rental amount, there is also an issue with meeting the material participation rules in some cases.

Material Participation

A passive activity loss can be deducted (provided you meet the other income requirements) as long as you have material participation in the property. In some cases this is a real problem for vacation homes. For example, the courts have consistently found that taxpayers cannot materially participate in a condominium hotel activity not located in their immediate vicinity. Because a vacation condo usually has full-time staff, taxpayers have to prove they materially participated, other than as "investors" for at least 500 hours.

In one tax court case, Professor Scheiner was a board member of the board that oversaw the operation of the condominiums. This constituted investor participation, but, according to the court, this failed to provide material participation.

In another case, Robert Serenbetz could not deduct rental activity losses involving an out-of-state condo partnership because he did not materially participate. Full-time condo staff managed the day-to-day rental operations. His activities of preparing tax returns, reviewing budget, attending partner meetings, and paying bills were considered investor activities. That meant he didn't get the passive activity loss write-off, either!

Sometimes you can win, though. Mr. and Mrs. Pohoski convinced the court that they spent more time, 200 hours annually, than did their management firm in maintaining their condo. This meant that they met the 100-hour test. Key to the decision was the rejection of the IRS's contention that the time the front desk was open should count as time for the management firm.

SELLING A VACATION HOME

Now let's jump back and assume that your second residence is actually a second home. You're ready to sell the property; now what?

Vacation homes end up in a kind of tax loophole limbo. They won't qualify for the principal residence exclusion, and they don't qualify for a like-kind exchange.

There are two possible strategies: (1) Convert the property to a rental first and then do a like-kind exchange, or (2) move into the property for two years and then sell the property for a tax-free gain exclusion. If you do decide to switch principal residences, remember that you can't do it more often than once every two years.

One More Loophole Strategy for Vacation Homes

Here's one more strategy that might work, in the right circumstances. Occasionally, we'll run into clients who have a lot of money sitting in their pension funds and who are nearing retirement. One idea is to have the pension fund buy the home where they eventually want to retire. The pension rules will not allow them to live in the house while the pension owns it. But once they are ready to move, the pension can distribute the home to the taxpayers (it will be taxable if it's a regular pension or nontaxable if it's a ROTH) as their home. They've just accessed nonproductive pension funds to build their eventual dream home.

ACTION STEPS

1. Do you have, or soon plan to have, a second home?

2. Is your strategy to have a second residence or a rental property?

3. What changes (if any) do you need to make to ensure that you get the proper classification for the property?

4. What action steps do you want to take immediately?

PART IV

Creative Real Estate Investors

Chapter 12

CREATIVE WAYS TO CONTROL A PROPERTY

CREATIVE BUYING STRATEGIES

I f you have attended real estate seminars, or participated in any online real estate chats, you've probably heard of creative ways to buy properties. The way you buy the property will determine the tax treatment and the accounting requirements. In the next five chapters, we discuss the primary ways you can buy real estate and how to account for the transactions.

Leasing

The technique of leasing from a seller and then re-leasing the property is also known as a *sandwich lease*. You haven't bought the property and you haven't sold the property. The key distinction between leasing and buying is often in the contract that you write with the seller. If you aren't certain if you've bought or leased a property after reading this chapter, review the contracts with your attorneys.

In an ideal world, you should have a clear idea of HOW you

are buying the property plus WHY you are buying it before you buy. And, of course, the WHY of buying it includes what on earth you're going to do with it once you've got it!

Buying

In this case, when we use the term *buy*, we mean that you have received all the constructive benefits of ownership. Some examples of buying follow:

There is the very straightforward and simple buy, where you obtain new financing and buy the property through a title company or through an attorney, as appropriate for your state. In this case, you will need to know how to record the purchase from the closing document (HUD-1) and how to account for the monthly mortgage payments.

You might buy using a land contract or wrap-around lease. This means that you are making payments to the seller and the seller is responsible for an underlying mortgage. You might make the payments on both mortgages yourself. If that's the case, you now have two sets of mortgage payments to record each month. Or you might just make the payments directly with a down payment to the seller.

You might do an outright assumption where you take over the payments and your name is substituted for the seller. The accounting for that transfer would be the same as the first one. It's the same as obtaining new financing.

You might get a new loan and get the seller to carry back a note. In this case, you will make a monthly mortgage payment for the first note plus you will make periodic payments to the seller. You will have two sets of transactions to record.

You might assume the owner's financing by qualifying with the existing lender or buying from the owner "subject to" existing financing. In those cases, your accounting would be similar to the second one. On top of the payments for the underlying mortgage, you might have a separate payment to the seller as well if he carried back a note for part of the price.

Optioning

Another creative method of buying a property involves paying an option price for the right to own the property at a future date. In that case, you will likely be paying a lease payment on a monthly basis to the seller. You have not taken ownership of the property yet.

WHEN DID YOU BUY?

The important question in all of these creative real estate buying strategies is the determination of when you actually bought the property. Purchasing an investment property means that you can now begin depreciating the property. It also sets the start date for determining the holding period for a future sale.

When Did This All Begin? Carla's Story

Carla had bought a home with a lease option from the current owner. She then had leased it to a new buyer. Her buyer had faithfully made payments on the property for more than two years, and wanted to exercise his option on the property. So he exercised his option and paid (with the initial option amount) a total of $125,000 for the property. Of course, Carla had to first buy the property from her initial seller for her agreed-upon execution price of $95,500. The entire transaction occurred through a simultaneous escrow (each closed at the same time). She knew she would have to pay tax on the gain of $34,500, but since she had held the property for more than two years she had assumed that she would qualify for long-term capital gains treatment.

But after we reviewed her transaction, she learned that she actually hadn't bought the property until the day of the simultaneous escrow. Her holding period wasn't the two years that it had been rented. Her holding period was about a minute. That meant she had to pay tax at her ordinary tax rate. Unfortunately for Carla, she had not understood the particulars of her real estate deal and had not had an expert review it. As a result, she now owed about double the tax that she thought she would have to pay, and she had already spent the money.

It's important to understand holding periods and buy/lease concepts, especially if you are involved in creative real estate techniques. The wrong strategy might just double your taxes! The first step is often simply determining whether you are buying or renting a property when you use creative real estate techniques in the deal.

BUYING OR RENTING?

If you are looking at leasing a property, first determine whether constructive ownership has transferred. There are many ways to buy a property: subject to existing financing, seller financing, and outright purchase. In each of these cases, the clock has started ticking on ownership.

Ownership is crucial to determining the following:

- Depreciation calculation—Who gets the depreciation expense and when?
- Deductibility of the payment—Is it comprised of interest and principal or is it all rent expense?
- Start date for a future sale—Is the gain from the sale of the property long-term or short-term?

The typical sandwich lease, where you lease from a seller and then turn around and lease to a future buyer, is a pure lease. There has been no transfer of ownership in a sandwich lease. Typically this type of contract gives you, the buyer, the right to exercise an option and buy the property. You will have ownership only when you exercise the option. So if you then sell the property on a simultaneous close, you will receive no depreciation, amortization of payments is a moot point, and the holding period for the sale is only a fraction of a day.

Purchases that call for "subject to" existing financing are considered purchases of the property. Purchases also include land contracts, land trusts, seller financing, and wrap-around leases.

It is possible to buy a property and not record a title transaction.

Assume you are buying 123 Calle de Verde from Immanuel Rodriguez, using a Land Trust. Mr. Rodriguez transfers the property into a Land Trust, a type of revocable trust, named

123 Calle de Verde Family Trust. There are three parties to a Family Trust—the beneficiary, the trustor, and the trustee. Initially, the beneficiary and trustor are Mr. Rodriguez. You will be the trustee. In another document that is not recorded, Mr. Rodriguez transfers his beneficial interest to you. You now make payments on mortgage, property taxes, and all other responsibilities of ownership. You can also lease the property. In all respects you are the owner, although the title does not show that. The title shows that the Land Trust is the owner. But you own the Land Trust, and for accounting and tax purposes, you are the owner.

Assume you are buying a property at 987 Riverview Drive from Mrs. Patel using a "subject to" agreement. In this case, you have paid Mrs. Patel something in addition to the mortgage and then are responsible for all payments on the mortgage. There are additional steps to this, such as becoming an additional insured with the insurance company. However, you are the owner of the property even though the sale has all been accomplished with nonrecorded documents.

Creative Real Estate Investing Techniques

The two main questions a creative real estate investor needs to ask themselves about a property are:

1. Who owns the property? If you are leasing the property, you do not own the property. Benefits of ownership have not transferred.

2. If you own the property, when did you buy it? When did the control actually transfer? The start date determines whether a real estate dealer issue might be involved and the tax rate to be applied to the gain.

ACTION STEPS

1. After reviewing this information on tax implications of using creative techniques to control property, what one new insight do you have regarding buying property?

2. How could you use the information in this chapter in your own real estate investing?

3. What action steps do you want to put into place to maximize the benefits of building your real estate investment portfolio?

Chapter 13

CREATIVE TECHNIQUES TO PUT MONEY INTO YOUR POCKET

WHAT ARE YOU GOING TO DO WITH THE PROPERTY?

fter you've bought the property, or hopefully before you've bought it, you'll need to decide what you want to do with the property. You could develop it, live in it, rent it, sell it, or give it away.

RENTAL OR SALE OF PROPERTY

This section deals primarily with the rental or sale of property. However, it's not quite as simple as you might think when you examine whether the disposition is actually a sale or a rental.

First, though, consider whether you have created a clear and definite rental. Do you have a tenant for your property? Does that tenant have any future (or current) right of ownership, or do they simply have the right to use the property for a specific purpose and for a specific time frame? If the tenant simply has the right to use the property, it's a rental.

It's also fairly clear when you've done a straightforward sale. You had a close on the property through a title company or an attorney, and, as a result, the new owner now has title for the property. If that's the case, then skip this section entirely and go directly to Chapter 16—Accounting for the Sale.

CREATIVE REAL ESTATE DISPOSITIONS

It's easy to know what to do in the case of the clear-cut rental or sale. In the creative real estate world, though, creative and imaginative ways are often used to dispose of property. The names for these methods aren't generally reliable in determining the proper tax treatment.

For accounting purposes, there is really one question to be answered: Did you sell the property or not? You might receive a flow of income for many years under either case, so that is not a good way to determine the answer. The IRS does provide some guidance on this, though.

It is critical to determine whether the disposition of the property is really a rental or a sale. With a sale, you would have to pay tax on the gain resulting from it. And you would lose the depreciation benefit of ownership. On the other hand, the buyer now receives the benefits of ownership. They would have the interest expense deduction for either a principal residence or as a real estate investment. If it is a real estate investment for them, then they would receive the depreciation benefits.

On the other hand, if it is really a long-term rental, then you would continue to have the depreciation expense and the interest expense item. The income you receive would be rental income. If any of the payment you receive on a monthly basis will go toward the purchase price, then that is considered a payment toward the exercise price. That payment would not be immediately taxable.

And finally, the question of when you sold the property determines whether a like-kind exchange is possible. For example, if you have a long-term rental for which you have sold an option to purchase, the sale counts on the day that the exercise price is fully paid. On that day, you have all your cash and the clock starts ticking for the like-kind exchange. You can then buy another property with your tax-deferred proceeds.

On the other hand, if you sold the property on a long-term basis under which you receive payments over time, you have an installment sale. If your buyer pays you off in the future through a refinance, you will have cash but will have missed the opportunity for a like-kind exchange. The time frame of 180 days is likely to have passed and, at any rate, the payments you received will most likely not be received through an Accommodator.

Comparison of Rental versus Sale

Benefit	Rental	Sale
Mortgage interest deduction	Landlord (You)	Buyer (Not You)
Depreciation	Landlord (You)	Buyer (Not You)
Property tax deduction	Landlord (You)	Buyer (Not You)
Wealth growth potential	Landlord (You)	Buyer (Not You)

When it comes to tax planning, the Rent to Own program, which qualifies as a rental, has more advantages.

165

Lease or Sale?

In a Private Letter Ruling, the IRS states that there are four key factors in determining whether a sale has occurred:

1. The amount of and right to the purchase price is fixed and unqualified.
2. The obligation to convey title on the final payment of the purchase price is absolute.
3. The vendee (buyer) has taken possession or has the legal right to possession.
4. The vendee (buyer) has otherwise assumed the benefits and burdens of ownership.

We're also told in this Private Letter Ruling that no one single factor is controlling. It is necessary to look at each of these items to determine if a sale has occurred. In other tax court cases following this 1980 Private Letter Ruling, it was determined that #4 is critical in determining whether a sale has occurred.

These items are next discussed in more detail:

- The amount of and right to the purchase price is fixed and unqualified. If the price is fixed and unqualified, it indicates a sale in the year. Both authors have used the Rent to Own method for disposing of property. This method creates a rental, not a sale. The option price is generally set for either two or three years out. It adjusts to the market value every two or three years, since we agree to renegotiate the price if all payments are on time and the property passes an inspection. If the tenant–buyer does not wish to exercise the option at the end of the allotted time, the tenant–buyer loses their initial option payment, along with the portion of each

166

rental payment that was to be attributed to the exercise of the option. The tenancy is ended, and the buyer is required to vacate the premises.

On the other hand, a land contract, wrap sale, or installment sale is a sale. There is also a popular method that calls itself a "30 year purchase option." The reasoning is that the tenant–buyers are TRYING to turn the contract into a sale, because the tenant–buyers would then get the tax benefits of ownership. Of course, the seller then loses that benefit.

■ The obligation to convey the title on final payment of the purchase price is absolute. This might be a difficult point to win if you want to keep the rental benefits. But, of course, there is no one controlling factor in determining the rental/sale question.

One idea, though, is to make use of the court's determination that if there is a significant detriment to exercising this right, then the point might not be proven. For example, you might be able to prove that a prepayment penalty is a significant detriment to early exercise of the option.

■ The vendee (buyer) has taken possession or has the legal right to possession. The arguments for the second and third are very similar.

■ The vendee (buyer) has otherwise assumed the benefits and burdens of ownership. A court case has further determined that there are eight items to consider under this fourth step.

1. Right to possess the property.
2. Responsibility for insuring the property.
3. Right to rent the property and keep the profit.
4. Duty to maintain the property.
5. Bear the risk of loss or damage to the property.

6. Obligation to pay taxes, assessments, and charges against the property.

7. Right to improve the property without the seller's consent.

8. Right to obtain legal title at any time by paying off the contract.

After you and your advisors have reviewed that information, determine what type of disposition you have. If it's a sale, then it will be treated as an installment sale. Hopefully, you're not a real estate dealer and will be able to take the pro-rated installment sales tax treatment.

If it's a rental with an option, such as with the Rent to Own Program, then you have a bit of a hybrid. It's still a rental, but there are likely some other items to track.

ACCOUNTING FOR THE RENT TO OWN PROGRAMS

There are a few differences in accounting for the Rent to Own Program from a regular rental. The key differences are:

- Initial option payment.
- Ongoing option credits (the monthly amount we attribute to the final sales price).
- Impound accounts.
- Surrender.
- Exercise.

Initial Option Payment

The initial option payment is not treated as income until either the renter exercises the option or surrenders the option and moves out. It is first held in a kind of tax limbo until the final outcome is determined.

Ongoing Option Credits

Your contract likely calls for an amount that will be credited toward the future purchase of the property on a monthly basis. Our contracts, for example, state that an amount of around $100 will be credited toward the purchase if the payment is made early. An on-time or late payment does not qualify for that credit. This option credit is not considered income until the tenant–buyer buys the property or walks away.

Impound Accounts

In some rental option contracts, the renter is responsible for the property tax and insurance for the property. This amount is collected on a monthly basis from the renter and held by the owner for the payment. If either the insurance or property tax goes up, then the renter will have a rental increase to cover the amount. This is similar to an impound account that the mortgage company would keep for you. These schedules can be kept both to check the mortgage company (always a good idea!) and to track the renter's payments to you. In addition to the schedule, you will need to make an adjusting journal entry for the impound amount received.

Surrender

At the end of the option term, a renter can either buy the property or walk away. In this case, let's assume that the renter has decided to walk away from the property and leave behind the initial $5,000 option payment plus the $1,500 additional option buildup. The owner now has a total of $6,500 considered to be ordinary income.

You may find that reimbursing some of the deposit or option buildup can facilitate an easy end to her tenancy. We find that for the price of a few thousand dollars we often can get a huge benefit! One tenant even completely landscaped the front yard in exchange for a return of $4,000 of the option payment. And the property was absolutely spotless when we got it back.

Exercise the Option

Sometimes the renters exercise their option and buy the property. In that case, the option deposit will go toward the purchase of the property. Typically, the renter is buying it through a refinance, so there will be a standard HUD-1. You will need to report to the title company or attorney handling the closing how much in deposits you have received. That is the amount of the option account plus any balance in the impound account. When you receive the HUD-1 after the close of the property, you will see a line item showing the amount you reported. Your entry should debit the impound account and the option account for the amount shown in the deposit. Otherwise, the entry would be done exactly like any other entry to record a sale from the HUD-1.

ACTION STEPS

1. After reviewing the information in this chapter, are there any new creative real estate techniques you might use in your current or proposed rental programs?

2. How could the concept of delaying income tax on option payments help your current tax situation?

3. What action step do you want to commit to regarding your own personal real estate investing?

PART V

Easy Accounting for Real Estate Investors

Chapter 14

ACCOUNTING FOR THE BUY

GAINING CONTROL OF A PROPERTY

The chapter heading is Accounting for the Buy, but if you're using creative real estate investment techniques, you might find that you actually are leasing, not buying, a property. If after reviewing Chapter 12, Creative Ways to Control a Property, you determine that you actually have leased a property, then the next section is for you. Otherwise, you can skip ahead to the section after this one, on buying the property.

LEASING A PROPERTY

Let's assume that you have discovered that you are actually leasing a property. We'll also assume that you are leasing the property to another person. That way, at least, you have cash flow. Otherwise, you just have an expense.

As we have discussed, there are *straight leases* and *option leases*. One is a straightforward contract for specific use for a specific time period, while the other also contains an option to purchase the leased property. An option lease usually involves payment of an additional amount as consideration for the tenant receiving the option to purchase the property.

Accounting/Tax Issues for Leasing

The additional lease option payment is an asset that is held until you purchase the property or walk away from the deal. If you purchase the property, the option becomes part of the down payment for the property and will adjust the purchase price. If you walk away, this becomes an expense for your real estate business.

BUYING THE PROPERTY

On the other hand, let's look at what happens if you have bought the property. There are a number of ways to buy a property, but regardless of the way you buy it, you still need to calculate and record the same items. These items are:

- Basis in the property.
- Costs related to the purchase.
- Initial impound account balances.
- Other asset and liability accounts related to the purchase (such as insurance).
- Date of the purchase.

Outright Purchase

An outright purchase is the simplest to record and is also the easiest transaction with which you can find advisors to help you.

This is the type of sale that accountants and bookkeepers are taught in school. Make sure you give a copy of your HUD-1 settlement statement to your bookkeeper to make the needed entry.

Subject to Purchase

A "subject to" purchase occurs when you take over a seller's loan. In other words, you buy the property "subject to" the existing loans. You then make payments directly to the lender on behalf of the seller, make payments directly to the previous owner, or make payments to an intermediary.

Most loans have an impound account for property taxes and insurance. This impound account is held by the mortgage company and may be as much as one year or more worth of these expenses. It is really an asset that goes along with the property.

We suggest that you have the impound account reviewed and calculated when you take over a loan. Also, make sure you determine exactly who gets the value of the impound account. This could be an asset worth thousands of dollars, and many people simply forget that it exists. Most contracts do not specifically discuss how to handle the impound account. Make sure you have a good understanding of the deal so there is no confusion later.

Land Trust

Some creative real estate programs teach you to set up a land trust when you take over a seller's financing. The strategy is fairly straightforward. Let's assume that you and John Smith come to an agreement regarding your taking over his mortgage loan payments. You will pay him $1,000, catch up his past due payments, and then assume his loan on a subject to basis. The goal with the land trust is to facilitate this transfer in a manner that doesn't trigger the due on sale clause of the mortgage company. We showed you how this could be done at the end of Chapter 12. By making the land trust the owner of the property, and then transferring ownership of the land trust, the actual title on the property doesn't change.

Seller Financing

Another creative method for purchasing a property is with the use of seller financing. This may be done in conjunction with an existing or new mortgage. For accounting purposes, make sure you keep track of all loans for which you are responsible.

Some of the Money Came from Another Source

What do you do if some of the money comes from another source, such as an equity line of credit on other real or personal property? This is one of the few times that the answer will be dependent on how the rental property is owned.

For example, if both the asset securing the funds and the investment property are in your name, then the money from the investment is simply moved from one asset to another. On the other hand, if you borrow money on an equity line secured by your home, which is in your own personal name, and use it to buy an investment property, which is in an LLC, then you will need to either treat the money as a contribution of capital or a loan to the LLC.

Mixing Funds

Here is a fairly straightforward deal. Two friends get together to buy a property and one of the friends initially funds some of the costs. But just see how many steps can actually get involved as you start mixing up sources of funds.

Mei and Brenda buy a property together using conventional financing. Mei borrows against her home for the down payment. The agreement is that Mei will get that money back when they eventually sell the property. Brenda made the payments on the mortgage until they got a renter in the property.

It's now the end of the year and they are trying to unravel what they have done. First, they need to figure out what the deal is: How will they be compensated? What is the requirement for putting money into the project?

Initially, the property was just owned as tenants in common. Amounts advanced were calculated as loans due the joint venture and the basis was recorded. Later they formed an LLC to hold the property and transferred the records over.

Mei personally recorded the $50,000 amount drawn as an equity line on her personal books as a Note Receivable personally. It is now also a Note Payable on the books of the LLC.

On an ongoing basis, Mei would make the payment on the equity line personally and then the LLC would reimburse her for the expense. She would not take advantage of the interest expense as a deduction on her return. The deduction is now an expense of the LLC, of which she is part owner. The LLC files a tax return (Form 1065—U.S. Partnership Return) at year end. Schedule K-1s are prepared as part of this return. These schedules are given to the individual owners to be reported on their personal tax returns.

Brenda made the $1,200 per month payments from her cash. So she records on her personal books the cash outflow as a Note Receivable (N/R).

(Continued)

The LLC would record the payments made on its behalf as broken down by the amortization schedule. You would need to determine the principal and interest portion (from the amortization schedule) and the impound account amount for each payment made. For purposes of this example, we assume that the impound account is $100 and the principal portion is also $100. The interest portion is $1,000. Remember that the principal and interest portion would change each month when the principal balance is declining.

Note: If you want even more details on how Mei and Brenda recorded these transactions, go to www.DolfandDiane.com for a complete listing of the journal entries they made for the preceding steps.

Amortization of Note

Unless you have an interest-only note, you will need to separate each payment into interest and principal. It is also possible that the payments will include taxes and insurance (in which case the loan is called PITI—principal, interest, taxes, insurance) and perhaps even PMI (private mortgage insurance). These amounts would also have to be recorded on a monthly basis as the loan payments are recorded.

To calculate all the components, you will need an amortization schedule. We use the Tvalue program (available at www.timevalue.com for $150). I find this is the easiest way to create a printed amortization schedule, which we keep handy for each property we buy.

Check Your Mortgage Company!

The impound account amount is typically constant for one year. Most mortgage companies reassess the impound account balances on an annual basis.

Mortgage companies frequently buy and sell mortgages from other companies. It is becoming common practice for mortgages to sell between mortgage companies multiple times in a year. You don't have to give your permission to have this sale happen. In fact, you might not find out until after you've already written your check to the old place!

If your mortgage is sold during the year, be careful to ensure that the impound account balances are accurately transferred when the mortgage is sold. Review the impound account balance of each transaction to make sure the correct amount of credit had been transferred between mortgage companies.

Land versus Building

You will need to record portions of the real estate you purchased separately. Typically, the land and the depreciable portion of the building are recorded separately. If you hold your property within a business structure (and we strongly recommend that you do!), you will need to separately report the land value from the depreciable portion on the tax return for the entity.

Diane's firm is frequently asked about strategies for calculating the land value. Since land is not depreciable, you will want the lowest value legally and reasonably possible.

You will also need to value the personal property items

(chattels) of your purchase separately. The personal property items include the air conditioner, refrigerator, garbage disposals, and the like. The personal property items are not recorded on the financial statement separately. These valuations are held on a "subsidiary" schedule, which is used to calculate depreciation for the tax return. After the depreciation is calculated, the entry is made on the financial statement for the sum of all assets per property.

HUD-1

The HUD-1 settlement statement will show a number of costs when you buy the property. You will need to examine each line item to determine what is currently deductible and what must be capitalized (added to the basis). Here are some hints:

REAL ESTATE TAXES   Usually the property tax owed by the seller at the time of sale is credited to you on the HUD-1 Settlement Statement. Those taxes paid are part of your basis. You cannot deduct them as a current expense item.

SETTLEMENT COSTS   You must generally capitalize the settlement and closing costs associated with buying the property. Some examples of these types of costs are:

- Abstract fees (abstract of title fees).
- Charges for installing utility services.
- Legal fees (including title search and preparation of the sales contract and deed).
- Recording fees.
- Surveys.
- Transfer taxes.

- Owner's title insurance.
- Any amounts that the seller owes that you agree to pay, such as back taxes or interest, recording or mortgage fees, charges for improvements or repairs, and sales commissions.

Following are some items that would be current expenses for your real estate investment:

- Hazard insurance premium.
- Rent for the property prior to closing (paid by you).
- Utility costs.

WHAT RECORDS TO KEEP AND WHY

Real estate has some very definite requirements for records. If you're planning to be a serious real estate investor, then plan on keeping good track of records as you go. Often the biggest challenge that new investors have is with keeping good, accurate records. If you don't have good records, you might be unable to prove your deductions and then lose them in a subsequent audit, or if you are sued, be unable to prove that you really are running your investments as a business. Either way—you lose! Good records can protect you against those problems.

There are four types of record systems that we recommend: (1) temporary files, (2) permanent files, (3) financial statement files, and (4) backup for real estate professionals to prove the hours you have spent in each activity.

Temporary File

There will be income and expenses for your properties every year. For ease of use with your accounting system, keep the backup copies in alphabetical files that are closed and put away each year after your tax return is prepared.

As you pay an invoice, we recommend that you note on your copy the following information:

Date paid.

Check number.

Amount paid.

We have a rubber stamp that is used to stamp each invoice that has these items and then we draw a line. This prompts the accounts payable clerk to complete each line. The invoice copy is then filed alphabetically by the vendor name.

If you don't have a lot of invoices each year, you might just want to create file folders with A–C, D–F, and so on. In this way, you can quickly find your reference information and not have to set up a lot of files as you go.

Be careful of expenses that end up being capitalized. These are expenses that actually represent improvements to the property. For example, a room addition would be an improvement. Invoices representing additions to basis (capitalized expenses) should not be filed with your temporary files. Instead, these need to be filed with your permanent files.

At the end of the year, begin a new set of file folders, and start filing current invoices in those folders. For part of the year you will probably have two sets of files—the past year (for the tax return that hasn't yet been filed) and the current year. Make sure you have room in a filing cabinet for those files.

After your tax return is filed, take your previous year's temporary files and store them in a separate box. We typically recommend that you retain these records for five years. However, you may want to keep them for 10 years in case there is ever a lawsuit. Clearly label the box with the year so you know when you can shred the documents.

Permanent Files

Your permanent files are those files that you will keep "active" for long past the tax year. These are items related to ongoing issues, such as the basis for the property and underlying notes, and capitalized costs, such as additions as well as information related to the business structure in which you hold the property, if applicable.

The basis files will include documents, such as the closing statements upon the sale of the property, any previous property owned (such as a like-kind exchange that was performed) that affects the basis, and invoices and contracts for improvements made to the property as well as any sales documents for portions of the property. These should be filed under the property name.

You will also want to keep files related to any agreements for property, such as the insurance policies, government notices (zoning and the like), rental agreements, and management agreements for each property in the permanent files.

Keep at least one file on each property for the mortgage information for the property.

If you have sold the property and continue to receive payments, keep records of all contracts with the rest of the files in the permanent files for as long as you have transactions with the property.

When you have sold the property and are completely paid in full, transfer all of your permanent files for the property to the temporary files. At the end of the tax year, these files will become part of the records kept at year end.

You will also need to keep permanent files for the business structure. For example, if you hold your property in an LLC, you will need to keep the documents related to the setup plus all of your annual reports and minutes. It is important that you keep all business structure paperwork handy. If you are ever sued, that's the first thing you'll need to produce. Failure to produce the necessary documentation might mean that you haven't run the business in a businesslike manner and put all of your other assets at risk.

Financial Statement Files

Most investors use a software program to track their income and expenses. Intuit's QuickBooks Pro (available at www.intuit.com for approximately $300) is commonly used with many real estate investors just starting out. This program allows clients to securely send their accounting data via the Internet to their CPA firm. The CPA can then look at the financial information at the same time that the client does.

Don't forget your computer system files. Consult with your computer support expert's advice for backups in your particular case. We generally follow the grandfather-father-son system of backups. In other words, we have three backup tapes that we use for backups. These are recycled through the series, so that we would always have three days of backup available. Additionally, we do a weekly backup that is taken and stored off-site.

Additionally, we recommend that you print the following reports after you have entered the year-end adjusting journal entries (AJEs) provided by your accountant:

Working trial balance as of the year end.

Balance sheet as of the year end.

Income statement for the year just ended.

General ledger—with all details.

Payroll records, full detail for all employees.

Bank statement reconcilement.

If you use the accounts receivable and accounts payable ledgers, print these out as of the year end.

Keep those reports with the other temporary files at year end. If you are audited for that year, the IRS auditor will ask to see copies of all of these financial reports. So, it is important you keep clean copies of these, without any notes written on them that you wouldn't want prying eyes to see.

ACTION STEPS

1. Review the information on leasing versus buying. Have you used some creative buying techniques that now need review?

2. For properties you currently own, review your current bookkeeping system. Do you have adequate documentation in case you are audited?

3. For properties you will buy, what systems do you want to put in place to verify that your accountant and/or bookkeeper will get the necessary information to properly record the transactions?

4. What other systems do you currently have that might need review after you have read this section?

5. What action steps do you want to put immediately into place to ensure good recordkeeping and proper accounting so that you can take advantage of all the tax benefits of your properties?

Chapter 15

ACCOUNTING FOR THE HOLD

RENTAL PROPERTY

I f you're looking for the best tax advantages from your real estate investments, then rental properties will give you that benefit. That's because the properties you hold have the ability to create paper losses. Of course, you need to be able to take advantage of those paper losses.

There is the standard rental of properties, with residential, commercial, or industrial tenants, and then there is the Rent to Own type of property where tenants have the option to buy the property at a predetermined price in the future. Both of these types of rental programs provide the same tax benefit to you as the owner—depreciation.

STANDARD RENTAL ACCOUNTING

Professional management companies generally follow a standard in the way that their financial statements are presented. Property management accounting software, such as Yardi, will produce financial statements in this format. If you will be managing properties for others, or working with investors, you will need to present the financial statements in the industry standard format.

Standard Financial Statements

The following is a standard financial statement format used by professionals. On the left is the title and to the right is the explanation. These are typically prepared on a monthly basis.

Title	Explanation
Gross income	Total income, if all units were rented.
Vacancy	Vacancy percentage.
Gross rents	Gross income minus the vacancy. This will equal the actual amount of rent you received.
Accounting	Accounting and bookkeeping costs.
Advertising	Cost of advertising.
Insurance	Cost of insurance.
Taxes	Cost of property and other taxes related to the property.
Legal	Cost of legal fees.
Professional management	Cost of property management.
Resident management	Cost of resident manager.
Office and telephone	Cost of the office and telephone.
Other	Miscellaneous.
Repairs and management	Cost of repairs and maintenance.

Trash	Cost of trash collection.
Utilities	
Gas	Cost of gas utilities.
Electric	Cost of electric utilities.
Water	Cost of water.
Sewer	Cost of sewer fees.
Other	Cost of any other utilities.
Total expenses	Total of all expenses.
Net operating income	Gross income minus total expenses.
Less debt service	Total of the mortgage payments.

Rental Financial Statement

The statement just shown is actually a hybrid of a standard financial statement, a combination of both a profit and loss (income statement) and a balance sheet. It is used to determine the cash on cash return and ROI (return on investment) calculations.

You (or your bookkeeper) will still need to create the typical financial statements when it comes to tax time. The entries will be fairly straightforward with a couple of unique points, which are covered in the following sections.

Amortization

You will need to separately record the principal, interest, and if applicable, impound portions of your monthly payments. Some lender statements will show the breakdown of principal and interest. Otherwise, you will need to run a loan amortization schedule to break out principal and interest.

Impound Accounts

It is not necessary to separately record and track your impound account. Your mortgage company will provide that tracking at least annually. Many companies now provide the impound account information on a monthly basis. As we said earlier though, mortgages are frequently bought and sold, and the impound account amount is often found to be incorrectly transferred. Make sure you double-check this account at least once a year.

Tenant Deposits

You will hopefully have deposits from your tenants before they move in. When you first purchase a rental property, you will likely also receive these deposits. As a side note, you might want to send letters to the current renters to verify the deposit amounts as part of your final due diligence process for the purchase.

These are liabilities, not income. When the tenant moves out, they will either receive some of the deposit back (in which case you charge the amount of the check you write against the tenant's deposit) or you will use that deposit to pay for cleaning and damages. If you receive the deposits for reimbursement of damages, then amounts become income.

Tenant deposits can become a powerful point of negotiation when you buy a new property. Let's say there is $50,000 in tenant deposits held by the seller. Your contract calls for these amounts to transfer to you at the sale date. The property will cost $1,000,000 and you have a loan for $800,000 promised to you. That means that you will need to come up with $200,000 in down payment. But you will get a $50,000 credit for the tenant deposits when you close. This amount directly reduces the cash that you will need to come up with to close the property. And best of all, it won't cost you a bit of tax to do it. In this case, the $50,000 is considered a future liability, not income. After all, the tenants could all move out, leaving their rented spaces in pristine condition, and you would owe the money back. In reality, it's highly unlikely that would occur, especially since you'll have made sure that there are good leases in place prior to purchase.

Depreciation

Many real estate owners who also do their own bookkeeping do not prepare depreciation schedules. Depreciation calculations can be a little tricky, especially in states such as California, which have not adopted the federal guidelines. In those states you have to keep a separate depreciation schedule for the state in addition to the federal schedule. Plus with the AMT hitting more and more Americans, there is yet a third depreciation schedule. We think it has become completely unwieldy to do the depreciation calculation without tax preparation software. And if you're dealing with state issues and alternative minimum tax, you'll likely need a good, and expensive, software program. We're right back to the recommendation of having your CPA give you the depreciation entries at year end.

Upon purchase, you will need to provide a breakdown of the personal property items within your property. Some jurisdictions require that you file this list with the fair market value with the taxing authority, as the personal property items are taxed at a different value from the structure. At the very least, your accountant should use such a list to calculate the various rates of depreciation. ChattelAppraisals.com provides a great starting point.

Additionally, you will need to inform your CPA at year end of any additions you have made to your property. It's very tempting to just code all maintenance and repairs to "repair" but you and your CPA will need to look at these items at year end to determine which can be expensed as deductions in the current year and which must be capitalized and then depreciated over time.

Repairs versus Capitalization

Repairs are currently deductible but capitalized expenses are depreciated over time. In an ideal world, all repairs would be expenses and everyone would get the deduction right away. Unfortunately, it's not that easy.

The IRS tells us that if a repair extends the life or adds value to an asset, then it is a capitalizable item. That, of course, can lead to a debate as to what extends the life of an asset. Ongoing maintenance is necessary to keep a property in good repair, and if you do the maintenance, the asset has a longer life. Based on that chain of logic, any maintenance should be capitalized. At least, that's the argument the IRS tried to use in a 2000 Tax Court case. Fortunately, the IRS was soundly defeated! And interestingly the Tax Court found it significant in this case that the maintenance work in question had been performed as preventive maintenance, not restorative maintenance. There weren't any problems yet, otherwise the Tax Court may have felt that the $100,000 worth of repairs should have been capitalized. The loophole here is to make sure you have a tenant in place in a rentable space, so that you are doing repairs to keep the tenant in place and happy. Otherwise, you might be considered a developer, which means you have to capitalize not only the improvements but also all carrying costs while you hold the property.

One strategy to create a repair for tax purposes, and not a capitalized item, is to have small increments of work done. For example, don't wait until the whole roof is shot and needs to be completely replaced. Replace it in sections. You can take preventive measures as you go.

The IRS has a list of items that must be capitalized, which include:

- Cost of acquiring the property.
- Cost of defending or perfecting the title.
- Amounts paid or incurred to add to the value or substantially prolong the useful life.
- Amounts paid to adapt property to a new or different use.
- Costs of constructing buildings, machinery and equipment, furniture and fixtures, and similar property having a useful life substantially beyond the end of the current taxable year.
- Costs of installing machinery, equipment, furniture and fixtures, and similar property.

OPTION PAYMENTS

As discussed earlier, the initial option payment received on a Rent to Own or other form of lease option program will not be immediately taxable. Likewise, the monthly option portion of the

---

Tax Loopholes for Landlords

The best tax breaks come when you hold a property. Be a landlord and pay less tax.

- Tenant deposits are not taxable income until the tenant leaves.
- Expense repairs wherever possible.
- Avoid capitalizing improvements.
- Maximize depreciation.
- Option payments received are not taxable income until the tenant/buyer either exercises or leaves.

---

monthly payment on a Rent to Own Program will not be immediately taxable.

MONTHLY BOOKKEEPING

We recommend that you or your bookkeeper complete a financial statement for each property on a monthly basis. This helps you see what is working and what is not, so you can make changes as needed, and it also helps your accountant with year-end tax planning.

ACTION STEPS

1. For property you hold, are you taking advantage of all possible loopholes for landlords?

2. Are you (or your bookkeeper) properly coding tenant deposits and option payments as non-income liability items?

3. Are you happy with the frequency of the financial statements for your rental properties?

4. What action steps do you want to take immediately?

Chapter 16

ACCOUNTING FOR THE SALE

SALE—HOW DO YOU GET YOUR MONEY?

There are basically two ways you can get your money when you sell your property—now or later. Of course, there's also "never" as a possible answer, but that usually leads to foreclosures.

If you are receiving payments over time, through a note that you have given on the property, you have an installment sale. When you sell a property with an installment note, you will still need to calculate the amount of gain from the property and to do that you'll need to know the sales price, cost of selling, and basis.

Of course, sometimes you have a plain old-fashioned sale where you sell your property and get your money. Even in that case, you will still need to calculate your basis, your gain, and record the sale of the property.

Basis

In the simplest terms, the *basis* is what you paid for a property. Of course, that is affected by the items that need to be capitalized with the purchase and for any improvements that you have made on the property. Plus, you will need to reduce your basis by any partial dispositions of the property (i.e., selling off one part of your land and keeping the house and the rest of the land). If you have rolled over your basis from previously owned real estate through either a pre-1997 home sale or a like-kind exchange, use that basis amount.

This is one place where keeping good records will help you. If you don't know what the basis is, you'll need to figure it out. Unfortunately, if you don't have the backup documentation for proof, you might lose some basis. Lower basis means less deduction, and that means more tax.

INHERITED OR GIFTED PROPERTY   If you have received property, or even partial interest in property, through gift or inheritance, your basis will be calculated differently.

If you received a gift and paid gift tax, you will have a stated basis that the IRS knows about. If, on the other hand, you received Mom's house when she deeded it over to you without consulting a CPA or attorney, you have a tax mess. A gift in excess of the annual gift tax exclusion amount is taxable at gift tax rates. Most likely in this case, you will owe gift tax and then have your basis established. This is a case where you need an experienced estate planning CPA or attorney to help you determine how to fix the situation with the least amount of tax.

On the other hand, if you inherited property prior to 2010, you will have a "stepped-up" basis in the property. There will be a valuation made at the time of death that then sets the value for you to inherit the property. The estate tax laws are undergoing fierce scrutiny and are likely to be changing soon. More than any other area of tax law, this is one area on which you will want to stay current and have competent advisors who also stay current on the tax law.

Calculate Gain

The first confusion that often occurs for a first-time real estate seller is their failure to understand that the cash you receive has nothing to do with the gain you will pay tax on.

The *gain* is the sales price minus the cost of sales minus the basis. The cash you receive is the sales price minus the cost of sales minus the outstanding loan. Unless your loan equals the basis, and it seldom does, you will pay tax on an amount that is different from the cash you receive.

The basis you have previously calculated actually has two different components when you are calculating the gain. First, you need to "recapture" the depreciation that you have previously taken on the property. So if your basis was $100,000 minus $20,000 worth of depreciation on a property you sold for $150,000, the following would be true:

Basis	$ 80,000
Sales price	150,000
Total gain	70,000
Recaptured depreciation	$ 20,000
Capital gains portion	$ 50,000

There are two different ways that the recaptured depreciation may be taxed. For real property, the portion of accelerated depreciation that exceeds the straight-line depreciation is taxed at a special 25 percent tax rate. The portion of depreciation that would have been taken under the straight-line rate will be recaptured at the ordinary tax rate. Non-residential real estate must be depreciated over 39 years using the straight-line method, so only recaptured depreciation will just be taxed at ordinary rates.

CARRYING BACK A NOTE

Recently we've seen a lot of creative real estate seminars promoting the method of carrying back a note when you sell property or wrapping existing financing. In either case, you have now sold property and taken back a note. You are selling using an installment method. There are some specific tax and accounting issues for the installment method. In general, the best reason (and perhaps the only reason) to do an installment method sale is because you are actually using financing to sell the property. For some reason the property can't qualify for a loan, or your buyer won't be able to qualify. Make sure they pay a premium for the privilege of tying up your money. Plus, make sure you have taken all of your tax consequences into account. The box on the opposite page is a true-life story of one brand-new creative real estate investor who made some very costly mistakes.

The moral of the story is make sure you have good advice and a good understanding of the tax rules before you start a new venture. You might end up with a good deal, just like Neil did, but find out or the taxes will bury you!

Depreciation Recapture for the Installment Method

The IRS requires you to account for, and pay tax separately on, recapture of previous depreciation. Depending on how you initially depreciated the property and the type of property, you will pay at either the ordinary income tax rate or 25 percent.

When you calculate the taxable income on your installment sale, remember that you will need to first pay at the depreciation recapture rate until it is paid in full. So if part of the gain is taxed at 25 percent and part is at the capital gains rate of 15 percent,

Real Life Example—Dealing in the Real World

Neil was excited with the gains he had made in real estate over the past year. He'd heard that as a real estate investor he got tremendous tax advantages, such as something called "real estate paper losses" so that he received cash and didn't have to pay tax. Plus, he knew, because everyone had told him, that the world's wealthiest people created their wealth with real estate (or held their wealth in real estate).

One year before, Neil had been fed up with the losses that he kept experiencing in his 401(k) plan, so he took the bold move of pulling out the remaining $100,000 that was left. The 401(k) pension administrator told him there would be a penalty and tax due, but that didn't bother Neil. He knew he could make more money on real estate and so took the money anyway. The remaining $100,000 balance was down from the high of $300,000 three years prior.

Neil then went to a seminar about real estate "flips"—buying property, doing minor renovations, and then selling them for a quick profit, and he was hooked! He also learned about selling property on land contracts to people who had bad credit. On one deal alone, he had bought a property for $80,000 and put about $5,000 into fixing it up. His payments on the loan were only $479.64 for the principal and interest, with interest at his low interest rate of 6 percent. He then starting looking for someone to buy the property and he quickly found someone. He tried negotiating a sale for a

(Continued)

Real Life Example *(Continued)*

price of $100,000 with an interest rate of 8 percent and the prospective buyer flipped out! They were certain that the bad credit they had shouldn't mean that they had a higher interest rate. Neil was very proud of the deal he ended up with—a sales price of $116,000 with interest rate of 6.5 percent. The funny thing was that his original offer would have meant a payment of $733.76, and the deal they ended up with had a payment of $733.20. Although the interest rate went down, the sales price went up, so their payment was about the same.

Neil had a cash flow of a little more than $253 per month and was very happy . . . until tax time. That's when Neil discovered the true tax cost of what he had done. He wasn't a real estate investor, he was a real estate dealer. The money he made from flips was subject to self-employment tax, plus he had to pay the ordinary tax rate and could not take advantage of the capital gains rate. Plus, he had to deal with the penalty and taxes due on the 401(k) withdrawal, and to make it all even worse, he had to pay tax on the gains from the sale of the property. His tax bill ended up being:

Penalty and tax on 401(k)	$48,000
Tax on gain of property	15,000
	$73,000

Most of his original $100,000 investment went to taxes. In exchange he has only $253 per month cash flow.

---

you will first pay at the 25 percent rate until all the previously taken depreciation is used up.

REPORTING REQUIREMENTS IF YOU SELL ON THE INSTALLMENT METHOD You will need to track the interest that you receive from your buyer on an annual basis. This needs to be reported to the buyer via Form 1098 by January 31 of the year following.

IMPOUND ACCOUNTS FOR THE INSTALLMENT METHOD You will likely need to keep track of the impound account that your buyer is creating. On a monthly basis, the buyer will make payments to you that go toward the property tax and insurance. You will then make payments on a periodic basis for them.

Before You Sell

You will need to know the following before you can determine the amount of tax you'll pay on a property sale:

- Sales price.
- Selling costs.
- Basis.
- Holding period (long-term or short-term).
- Cash sale or installment sale.
- Amount of accumulated depreciation.
- Method used to calculate depreciation.
- Your ordinary tax rate.

FINAL WORDS ON THE SELLING OF PROPERTY

The biggest tax mistakes taxpayers make are when they sell a property and fail to understand what their taxable gain and the applicable tax will actually be. Spend some time planning for the taxes before you finalize your deal. Sometimes a little change you can make now won't cost the buyer anything but could save you a lot of headaches later.

ACTION STEPS

1. Do you anticipate selling any real estate property? If so, have you reviewed the gain, and how it will be taxed?

2. What action steps do you want to take immediately?

PART VI

Global Investing

Chapter 17

THE CASE FOR GLOBAL INVESTING

I f nothing else, this book so far should have convinced you that the tax laws as they relate to real estate in the United States are extremely complex, continually changing, and almost impossible to remember.

And the United States is by no means unique on this front! The tax laws in most other countries are similarly complex (and vastly different from country to country).

WHY INVEST IN OTHER COUNTRIES?

So why then could we possibly be suggesting that you should consider investing in other countries (or even only one other country) with completely different rules, when most of us are struggling to get a handle on even our own laws?

To answer this, we need to consider three elements:

- Your core profession.
- Leverage of time.
- Overriding benefits.

Your Core Profession

While we concede that the tax laws in the United States are extremely complex, we are not suggesting that you become an expert in real estate tax laws. Even if you spent 50 hours a week studying real estate tax law, you would still not know all there is to know, and, more importantly, you would have no time or energy left to find great real estate deals. Rather, we strongly recommend that you find real estate savvy bookkeepers and tax practitioners who can not only do your paperwork for you, but who can advise you on new changes to the law that you can take advantage of. That leaves your time free to do what you are good at and hopefully love doing: finding, negotiating, financing, and renting out lucrative real estate deals.

A great rally driver doesn't need to know how to repair his turbocharger; he is just good at driving efficiently. A great pilot needs to know how to handle a crisis situation, such as wind shear or an engine failure during flight, but he does not need to know how to repair a jet engine. Similarly, a great real estate investor does not need to know how to interpret, invoke, or comply with every nuance of tax law. Rather, the rally driver, pilot, and real estate investor all have teams of people who are specialists in areas that they are not necessarily experts in. You have to focus on what your core activity is and leave other experts to focus on what they are good at. That leads us to point number two.

Leverage of Time

In another book *An Insider's Guide to Making Money in Real Estate Investing*, we discuss the importance of leverage of time, where we get other people to willingly do what we either are no good at doing, or have no time or inclination to do.

Successful people do not do everything themselves. Rather, they surround themselves with teams of people, each specialists in their own fields, who can enable them to focus on those things that they are experts at.

We even go on to describe how you can attract such a team of specialists. One central theme is to interview potential team members, to find out if they have the knowledge and drive to be part of your team. To this end, knowing which questions to ask can be very useful. Reading this book may be useful when you interview potential real estate savvy accountants. But we are not suggesting that you read this book once and then do all your accounting yourself.

The way we both operate, and what we encourage you to do, is to become sufficiently skilled in a subject so that you can discuss matters with your advisors with confidence, but still defer to their greater knowledge of the subject.

In other words, we do not recommend that you make all your own real estate tax decisions yourself and fill out and file your own returns. It is generally much smarter to save a lot of time, trauma, and possibly regrets by having experts perform 99 percent of the work for you, and you just remain the well-informed real estate investor who can focus on the task at hand: finding lucrative deals.

If it makes sense to use a tax expert in your own country, then it must make equally good sense to use tax experts in other countries. Learn the rudiments of the local tax laws, and then let the local experts fill out all the required forms so that once again you can concentrate on doing what you do best: finding lucrative deals.

In other words, not knowing the local tax laws is no real impediment to doing great deals in foreign countries.

Overriding Benefits

You may agree that you can hire tax experts to look after the rules and paperwork for you, but you still have reservations. Why spend time and money traveling to another country, with time zone differences, language barriers, cell-phone incompatibilities, strange customs, odd habits, weird food, and a propensity to drive on the wrong side of the road just to do a real estate deal, when there are more deals in your own back yard than you can possibly look at?

With this attitude, you should never do deals out-of-state, or even out-of-county, or, for that matter, out of your own town. In fact, why not just focus on your current street, and then you can save gas when collecting the rent, too?

Well, the counter on the domestic front is that other states may have capital growth rates that far outstrip the rate in your home state. There may be tax advantages (no state income tax or no transfer tax), structuring advantages (cheaper to run and maintain an LLC), demographic advantages (a burgeoning population that provides a steady flow of tenants), geological advantages (no earthquake zones, hurricane fears, or water shortages), or city advantages (no rent controls). And rather than its being a burden to go to inspect a rental property, visiting it once or twice a year may be fun. We are sure that many out-of-state owners of rental units in Las Vegas or California do not mind their tax-deductible inspection trips.

All the advantages just listed that justify domestic diversification also apply to international diversification. Other nations may have a combination of favorable capital growth, demographics, geology, available business structures, and taxes to make them worthwhile as possible investing destinations. For example, there are countries with one or more of the following: zero capital gains tax (it does not even exist on the statutes); a top personal income tax rate of 15.5 percent; unlimited deductibility of operating losses against other income (no matter what your income level); no transfer tax; and no death, inheritance, or estate tax. But the advantages do not stop there.

When you deal only in one country, then all your eggs are in one financial basket. Most people do not realize that the value of the United States dollar, when measured against a trade-weighted basket of foreign currencies, has gone down by more than 50 percent in the past four years. By investing abroad, you can start to spread your investment eggs so that your overall net worth will not rise and fall with the local tide.

Investing overseas can also be seen as an extremely patriotic thing to do. When you invest just within your own country, then in a sense any profits you make are just a redistribution of the existing wealth in the country. It is a bit like the government taxing one group of people to redistribute to another group. But when you invest overseas, and, assuming you run at a profit and bring money back into the country, then you are adding to the wealth of the country.

And the fact that you are investing abroad does not mean that you have to export a lot of investment dollars to those countries you choose to invest in. On the contrary, we strongly advise against taking one currency to another country to invest locally. Rather, borrow locally in the local currency. That way, you will never be caught out by an unfavorable shift in exchange rates against you.

This brings us to another point. Most people are attracted to the lure of international travel. They work hard, pay taxes, spend money on essentials such as food, clothing, accommodations, gas, insurance, and on nonessentials and then try to save whatever is left over so that every two or three years they can enjoy a vacation abroad using their tax-paid dollars. The international investor, on the other hand, can use his pretax income to fund trips abroad to inspect properties already held, meet with and check on property managers, refinance loans, and look for new deals. It is only what is left over after the trip that gets taxed.

We are so hooked on real estate investing, that when we go somewhere on holiday, we enjoy looking at local real estate deals. What is the difference between going on vacation and looking at real estate deals and maybe buying some, and going on a real estate buying business trip to the same location? More specifically, while you are having breakfast and looking at the waves crash in on the beach below your hotel, what, in that moment, is the difference?

The world is constantly evolving. Two generations ago it was very uncommon for people to travel to other continents, and immigrants often never returned to their country of birth. Today, we can zip around the world in less than a day, and be in instant cell-phone communication with just about anyone we want for cents per minute. As free-trade agreements and double-tax agreements between nations develop and expand, international travel, vacations, trade, and investing opportunities will increase exponentially. The question is, do you want to be experiencing it from interesting, exotic locations, or do you want to be observing it as you grow old in your hometown, knowing that everything you could possibly want to see in the world you can experience on television—no passport required, no inoculations, no time-zone changes, no jet lag, no airport delays, no customs officials, no travelers checks, just the humdrum of the same day lived over and over again?

As you have read throughout this book, there are many loopholes that the government provides to domestic real estate investors. These loopholes are not anomalies that the government will close as soon as they become aware of them! Rather, they are government-imposed incentives to help shape social policy. The government wants you to invest in real estate. And, would you believe it, banks want to lend you money to help you buy it, and there is a pool of tenants willing to pay you money to rent the properties.

Other governments similarly have incentives—loopholes—to encourage you to invest in real estate. And banks in those countries similarly want to lend you money, and there are also tenants there who want to rent from you.

To cap it all off, the respective governments have put their heads together to come up with formulas so that you will not be taxed twice—tax paid in one country will be credited toward your tax bill in the other.

Do the airlines have to give you free tickets as well? Come on, they are struggling as it is.

We are not suggesting that your first real estate deal should be abroad. In fact, doing your first deal in the city where you live is probably wise. But your twentieth or thirtieth deal . . . now that's another story.

ACTION STEPS

1. Pick a country that has always fascinated you. Start to conduct some preliminary research. Is it politically stable? Do they welcome foreign investors? What have capital growth rates been in the past? Is there a capital gains tax? What are top marginal tax rates? How graduated is the tax scale? Can you repatriate profits? Will banks lend to foreigners? What are average yields? What structures are available? Of course, some of these questions may require onsite investigations. Darn!

2. Know that for a property investor more than for any other profession, the world truly is your oyster.

3. Take a deep breath, and step into your local travel agency.

Meet Diane Kennedy

Diane Kennedy, the nation's preeminent tax strategist, is owner of D Kennedy & Associates, a leading tax strategy and accounting firm, and the author of *The Wall Street Journal* and *BusinessWeek* bestsellers, *Loopholes of the Rich* and *Real Estate Loopholes*.

Diane's extensive teachings have empowered people throughout the country to minimize their tax liabilities through the use of legal tax loopholes.

Diane has written for *The Tax Savings Report, Investment Advisor Magazine, Personal Excellence*, the Money & Finance section of *Balance* magazine, and *Healthy Wealthy n Wise*, where she has a regular column. She's been featured in *Kiplinger's Personal Finance, The Wall Street Journal, USA Today*, and the *Associated Press* and on *CNN, CNNfn, Bloomberg TV* and *Radio, CNBC, StockTalkAmerica*, and numerous regional TV and radio shows.

A highly sought-after international speaker and educator, she has dedicated her career to empowering and educating others about financial investments and the tax advantages that are available. Through Diane's knowledge and execution of legal tax loopholes in her business and real estate investments, she and her husband Richard are able to contribute to special life-changing projects and charities in the United States and third-world countries.

Diane provides critical tax law updates, advice on the latest tax loopholes, as well as tax-advantaged wealth-building resources on her web site: www.TaxLoopholes.com (821 North Fifth Avenue, Phoenix, AZ 85003, 1-888-592-4769).

Meet Dolf de Roos

Dr. Dolf de Roos began investing in real estate as an undergraduate student. Despite going on to earn a Ph.D. in electrical and electronic engineering from the University of Canterbury, Dolf increasingly focused on his flair for real estate investing, which has enabled him to have never had a job. He has, however, invested in many classes of real estate (residential, commercial, industrial, hospitality, and specialist) all over the world.

Today he is the chairman of the public company Property Ventures Limited, an innovative real estate investment company whose stated mission is to massively increase stockholders' worth. Over the years, Dolf was cajoled into sharing his investment strategies, and he has run seminars on the Psychology of Creating Wealth and on Real Estate Investing throughout North America, Australia, New Zealand, Asia, the Middle East, and Europe since the 1980s.

Beyond sharing his investment philosophy and strategies with tens of thousands of investors (beginners as well as seasoned experts), Dolf has also trained real estate agents, written and published numerous bestselling books on property, and introduced computer software designed to analyze and manage properties quickly and efficiently. He often speaks at investors' conferences, real estate agents' conventions, and his own international seminars, and regularly takes part in radio shows and television debates. Born in New Zealand, raised in Australia, New Zealand, and Europe, Dolf, with six languages up his sleeve, offers a truly global perspective on the surprisingly lucrative wealth-building opportunities of real estate.

To find out what you can learn from Dolf's willingness to share his knowledge about creating wealth through real estate, and to receive his free monthly newsletter, please visit his web site at www.dolfderoos.com.

Index